Find Your Landing Zone

Life Beyond the Bar

KEVIN McGOFF

Cover design by Sara Wadford/ABA Design

Printed in the United States of America.

27 26 25 24   5 4 3 2

Library of Congress Cataloging-in-Publication Data

Names: McGoff, Kevin P., 1953- author.
Title: Find your landing zone : life beyond the bar / Kevin McGoff.
Description: Chicago, Illinois : ABA Publishing, American Bar Association, 2023. | Includes bibliographical references. | Summary: "My intention in these pages is to tell you what I believe worked to get me moving and to encourage you to think about yourself for a few minutes. This book is not about making money or managing the funds you have in the bank, although I'll touch on the topic of finances. There are plenty of resources out there written by experts in the fields of personal finance, career change, and retirement planning for you to consult if you wish. I'm also not suggesting that you must drop everything and hire a career coach. Not everyone needs the same kick in the rear to advance them toward their goals"-- Provided by publisher.
Identifiers: LCCN 2023016798 (print) | LCCN 2023016799 (ebook) | ISBN 9781639053360 (hardcover) | ISBN 9781639053377 (epub)
Subjects: LCSH: Practice of law. | Law--Vocational guidance. | Lawyers--Finance, Personal. | Lawyers--Retirement--Planning.
Classification: LCC K115 .M44 2023 (print) | LCC K115 (ebook) | DDC 340.023--dc23/eng/20230724
LC record available at https://lccn.loc.gov/2023016798
LC ebook record available at https://lccn.loc.gov/2023016799

Discounts are available for books ordered in bulk. Special consideration is given to state bars, CLE programs, and other bar-related organizations. Inquire at Book Publishing, ABA Publishing, American Bar Association, 321 N. Clark Street, Chicago, Illinois 60654-7598.

www.shopABA.org

For Mom and Dad—Dottie and Jim.

What a great life we had
growing up on Durham Drive.

Thanks.

CONTENTS

PREFACE

Kevin "did nothing in particular and did it very well."[1] The words of W.S. Gilbert, written for the opera *Iolanthe,* pretty much described my 22-year-old self. Driving a pickup truck and supervising a team of vending machine delivery men could have been my life. I *was* doing nothing, and I was doing it *very* well.

Although I was taken by the attractive hourly wage and ample free time several nonchallenging jobs provided me, my wife, Patty, was not amused by my complacency. She got me off the couch, out of the truck, and back to school. I turned in my keys to the vending machines, hung up the blue shirt emblazoned with my name, and re-enrolled in college. I had already dropped out—twice—before my candy man career. Without my wife's influence, my high school diploma may have been my last.

I was taken aback some 40 years later when a friend, Scott King, observed that our "life plan" was alluring. My road from candy man to partner in a Midwest law firm to our life at present—cycling, traveling, and sometimes living in other lands—seemed "so strategic" to Scott. I burst out laughing when he marveled at our plan. *Strategy? Plan?* It never occurred to me that I had either. Surely he was joking. Why would anyone be interested in hearing about a plan I never thought I had?

Scott pressed on. He asked me to consider developing a program about navigating through a career in the law with the objective of one day living another life—a life where days are unencumbered by deadlines, billable-hours goals, and the demands of law partners, clients, and opposing parties—or perhaps a slowed-down version of a lawyer's life. The conversation morphed into that program and this book.

---

[1] Gilbert, W.S. *Iolanthe; or, The Peer and the Peri.* London: 1882.

I shared my nascent idea with lawyers and judges; friends, some attorneys and some not. I bent the ears of retirees and others up to their eyeballs managing their businesses. Everyone I asked graciously chimed in at my request for feedback. As is always the case when I've asked for help, I received better ideas than my own. I was given more books to peruse as resources. There were many "have you thought about this" conversations. Most of all, I was encouraged to proceed.

I almost didn't become a lawyer. Patty picked me up when bad grades struck my transcripts. Upon graduation, I accumulated a mountain of rejection letters from law firms in response to my résumé. She was there for me then, as well. Down the road, when cases blew up and I doubted my decision to take up law, she was quick to remind me, "You could have had the pickup truck."

If not for Patty, there would be nothing for me to tell you; if not for Scott, I would never have tried.

ACKNOWLEDGMENTS

To the many friends who helped me, I am grateful.

I know better than to recognize some who lent me a hand at the risk of forgetting others. I'll do it anyway. My apologies to those who gave me help that I fail to mention. Many have encouraged me, shared their thoughts, and offered support along the way. I'm thankful for the ideas gleaned from Ruth Bari, Tony Pickell, Ruell Fiant, Jack Turbiville, Steve David, Kathy Carr, Jim Reed, Sarah McShea, Terry Harrell, Kim Brand, Cari Sheehan, Anna Rappaport, Steve Terrell, Cynthia Sharp, Loretta Oleksy, Rob Dassow, Scott Yonover, David Prechtel, and Mohamed Bari. I borrowed from what I learned during conversations on the beach with Ron Ellis, Alfred Mijares, and Jeff Utschig. It was Mark Hershman who introduced me to the concept of taking the time to think about myself and planted the seeds of change. Thanks again, Mark.

My brothers, Jim and John, are great sounding boards. Siblings are never shy about delivering unvarnished opinions.

Sam and Di Rushing, Corinne Henderson, and John Sweeney invested much time offering their comments after reading a near-final draft. John Chamberlin, Nicole McGoff, and Michael Wright provided valuable insight for the chapter on finances.

Thanks to those who shared with me their stories of success: David and Debbie Yates, Steve Strawbridge, Debbie and Tom Gardner, John Sweeney, Jane Ruemmele, Kristi Dosh, and Dan and Noelle Gosling. There's great inspiration in what you've accomplished.

I had the good fortune to meet Doris Gallan when I attended her creative writing class in Puerto Vallarta several years ago. She graciously signed on to be my editor, coach, mentor, and taskmaster. Writing a book and drafting a brief are two different disciplines. The input, prodding, and work Doris provided as my editor were essential. Without it, this effort would read like a legal memo or be a pile of disorganized paper stuffed in a drawer awaiting the trash bin when another wave of downsizing overcomes us.

Donna Gollmer, Lorraine Murray, and Bryan Kay at ABA Publishing and the Senior Lawyers Division of the American Bar Association were gracious in giving me this opportunity. It is a memorable day when your first book proposal is accepted. I'm grateful they were willing to take a chance on my work.

INTRODUCTION

"Faith is taking the first step even when you don't see the whole staircase."

–Martin Luther King, American Baptist minister and civil rights activist (1929–1968)[1]

Where Are We Going? An Overview

I was part of a law firm management team, in various capacities, for more than 30 years. Early on, I ran my own practice. My solo practice evolved into a firm of 10 lawyers that I helped manage for more than 13 years. I was on the management committee and later served as general counsel (GC) in a firm of about 170 attorneys where the topic of retirement planning was periodically discussed. The succession plan for certain lawyers, so the quip went, was to have them dial 9-1-1 and request an ambulance as they fell over their desks. Unfortunately, this isn't all that far from the truth for some in our profession. There are lawyers who took their last breaths on the floor of a courtroom. I was determined that my exit would be more graceful.

"You have an active mind," observed Mark Hershman, a career coach I asked to help give me some direction. At age 54, I began working with him to plan the next part of my life. I wasn't sure what he meant by this comment. Upon hearing it, I was afraid that Mark didn't believe I could hold a thought. Perhaps I appeared to be a scatterbrain, coming across as if I had the attention span of a four-year-old. He explained that in his

[1] Martin Luther King Jr., September 12, 1962, speech to commemorate the centennial of the Preliminary Emancipation Proclamation (https://quoteinvestigator.com/2019/04/18/staircase/).

observation, a lot of ideas were flowing through my old noggin. They were in search of organization, a skill I was in need of sharpening.

It was the work with my career coach that forced me to bring purpose to my internal musings and occasional reflections about the future. Once given some direction, I was able to harmonize my ideas with serious thoughts about what I wanted to do in the years I remained upright. A plan began to unfold.

I discovered that much of what I learned from working with Mark had always been right in front of me. I had not taken the time to organize a strategy using advice and information that was at my fingertips. I was "too busy," the ubiquitous justification for inaction that is easy to use. I employed this excuse masterfully. But, in fact, I *chose* to be "too busy."

My intention in these pages is to tell you what I believe worked to get me moving and to encourage you to think about yourself for a few minutes. This book is not about making money or managing the funds you have in the bank, although, I'll touch on the topic of finances. There are plenty of resources out there written by experts in the fields of personal finance, career change, and retirement planning for you to consult if you wish. I'm not suggesting that you must drop everything and hire a career coach. Not everyone needs the same kick in the rear to advance them toward their goals.

I wish to inspire you to stop, look, and listen. Stop and make time to ask yourself, "Where am I headed?" Look at where you have been. Take clues from your past. They will help unlock ideas for you to put into play as you develop a plan for achieving your goals. Listen to those who have been down this same path and your advisors. By listening, you may hear a voice that beckons you to a change. While you listen, *hear* the advice from friends and family. They want you to be successful and satisfied in your life.

Let's Not Waste Any Time

Your time is valuable, it is not an abundant commodity. I get it, and I don't intend to waste it here. Setting aside time to read has, for some, become a seldom-enjoyed luxury. I have purposefully made this volume a short read. There was never room on my bookshelf for a 500-page tome about retirement planning or managing a mid-life crisis. In the midst of my life as a lawyer, I made no time in my day, week, or month for combing through much non-law-related material. There is no reason to add another fat, unread book to your nightstand. Less is more when it comes to encouraging busy professionals to take some time away from work and family to think about themselves.

You may very well have heard before some of what I am proposing. Perhaps you have given a passing thought to making some changes in your life. That is usual. If so, you have likely been exposed to some of what has been published about leading a balanced life, seizing hold of your career, lawyer wellness, or how to retire at age 40 without really trying. You will read a paragraph or more in these chapters and say, "I know that."

I found myself doing just that many times during the years as I was investigating what course I wished to chart. I often followed up my "I know that" moment by having a conversation with myself. It would go along the lines of, "Well, Kevin, why are you wasting time reading a book that is telling you what you already know? Get back to work. Bill somebody." Sometimes I concluded this brief conversation with myself by answering, "If I already knew that and thought it was good advice, why haven't I done anything about it?"

I read much on the subject of getting my act together, but I had to admit that I had not taken any action. I didn't quite know how to go about it. I was apprehensive about implementing any dramatic changes in my life. Why waste time when things were going well, even if my professional life had some elements that were stressful and not totally agreeable?

What Inspired You to Begin Thinking About Your Future?

I hope you found your way to this book because you are searching for a few ideas about being the architect of your future, rather than allowing yourself to be shaped by your surroundings. Perhaps you are attracted to the idea that with some thought, a bit of planning, and proper advice, you can carve a fulfilling path for yourself.

I fear that many successful professionals become stuck on a treadmill that will never stop. I've been there. We get overwhelmed by work and family obligations and, perhaps, commitments to church and volunteer organizations. Simply trying to enjoy a weekend or squeeze in a vacation becomes a hassle. Eventually, we can't get off the treadmill. The belt moves faster. We become too busy to focus on what the heck we're even doing.

What is the endgame? Who cares, I have a deal to close. We're in trial. I just need to get through today.

You may be sitting with this book in hand because you have some vision of the path to your goals and have taken a few steps toward bringing them to life. But you are also harried and being pulled in multiple directions. There may be nagging thoughts of inadequacy in some of your roles because you are so preoccupied with work. You question your abilities and capabilities in your work and your life. Am I performing at the highest level that I am able? Am I giving my family the time they need? If present, is my presence of high quality? I have no hobby; do I want one? I want more free time, but where would it come from?

This self-examination can result in neglecting to focus on a personal plan because our efforts and energy are redoubled to compensate for what we believe to be our shortcomings. The treadmill moves faster, but it doesn't go anywhere. Are you receptive to introspection and interested in applying effort to implementing a plan?

Maybe you're the consummate planner with multiple to-do lists. No task is too small to be cataloged, waiting for the satisfying stroke of your red pen to knock it off the list. Completed, vanquished, what is next on my list to be mastered?

Perhaps you are a bit restless. Generally satisfied with life and your career is going well, but periodically, a nagging concern that you are missing something crosses your mind.

If you're the curious type, you may always be investigating the world around you through books, documentaries, websites, and travel.

If you're a lifelong learner, you are likely searching for answers without having completely formulated the questions.

Maybe you're here for one of the above-listed reasons that got me started. Perhaps it is a combination of some of those on my list, or it's something unique to you. It's worth taking a minute to answer the question for yourself.

How I Got Started

Throughout my personal inquiry, I found myself at every one of these stages. As I began thinking about making a change, I used every resource I could find. I worked with my career coach Mark. Our financial planner, Michael Wright, was another valuable resource. I also did plenty of research. It was enjoyable because for a change it was focused on me and my wife, Patty. The planning had nothing to do with a client or the law firm.

At about age 52, I resolved that I would one day personally clean out my office. I had no plans to die at my desk. My strategy was to go out upright and on two feet. Of course, I was not able to drive downtown on day one of my plan to surrender my office entry fob and toss my parking garage pass to the managing partner. You can't just wake up one morning and walk away from your law job. We had three kids in college, a mortgage, and all the other normal responsibilities of life. I was reasonably satisfied with my work and had professional goals. I was not then prepared to decamp for seemingly greener pastures.

I didn't know what it was that I could do—or even wanted to do after lawyering. However, I wasn't too young to begin giving my future serious thought and to initiate deliberate planning for the day when clients, judges, and law partners were no longer priorities. It just didn't happen overnight.

I relied on the advice of others when tackling issues where expertise was needed. For about a year I worked with Mark, and Patty and I spent a little money investing in the plan with Michael Wright. I had a lot of support from Patty. In truth, the process was a team effort. We collaborated on the strategy and design of our plan to move beyond the point in our lives where work consumed most of our waking hours.

I talked to my father, mother, friends, relatives, and siblings about my ideas. I asked lots of questions. I read books and portions of books; sometimes, I only scanned the book jacket. I perused articles and performed Google searches. I even opened some government websites. There has been a lot written by others who have gone before us on this journey.

I visited the aisle mislabeled "self-help" in many bookstores. I took care not to be seen poking around in this aisle of my local bookshops. No need to have to fumble for an answer or suffer raised eyebrows if any of my colleagues saw me lurking there. I was prepared to jump in with the "gift for a troubled friend" statement before any questions if I was ever caught with something from the Chicken Soup series or a Tony Robbins in hand.

When in Denver visiting our daughters I was liberated. There I could spend an hour or two at a table in my favorite bookstore sipping a cup of tea without fear of being stigmatized as a devotee of the "self-help" aisle. Before me would be an openly displayed pile of volumes from which I hoped to learn what to do next in my life. This study pushed me toward the path of asking questions, gaining information, and beginning my formal quest to examine what was next for me.

Cues Are Motivators for Taking Action

One of my early mentors was a brilliant trial lawyer named Jim. Jim hired me one year out of law school and took me under his wing. He was well known for his work as a criminal defense attorney and divorce lawyer throughout the eastern part of Indiana. He had more business than he alone could handle. Jim worked incredible hours. He would be in the office before dawn. Some mornings, I would arrive at the office around 7:00 a.m. or 7:30 a.m. In winter, the sun had yet to rise. What I believed to be an early-morning start began with climbing up a set of stairs near Jim's office door. Jim had seen me pull into the parking lot and knew it was me clanging my way up the circular staircase to my third-floor office. As I hit the first step, Jim's deep voice would often bellow, "Good afternoon, McGraw," purposely mispronouncing the name of his new associate. Some days he'd already have put in two or three hours before I arrived. Jim would work until late in the evening, particularly during a trial. Saturdays and Sundays were often workdays as well.

Sadly, Jim died at the age of 58. He left the world just as his children were entering adulthood. His grandchildren would never take a ride on his boat, hear his great laugh, or listen to the tall tales he would have invented for them. He missed out on a great part of his life. Jim taught me a lot about being a lawyer. I would never have developed my skills as a trial lawyer without his guidance. He also provided me with an important cue early in my life as a lawyer: there is more to life than work. I was a bit slow at that age. It was many years before I fully appreciated this important cue.

It's a Winding Road

The route to a different pace and place in life was never a straight-line path for me. It was always a bit meandering. There were times when things didn't go smoothly. I had to switch gears and I changed directions a few times. There were false starts and disappointments. I modified the goals that I had set, and I restarted this effort several times. Patty and I enjoyed the process of planning, much like we did when mapping out a vacation.

I was resistant to the concept called retirement. My endgame was never to attain nirvana in the form of leisurely days on the golf course at Sun City. I don't, to this day, see myself as being retired. Retirement is defined as: "to withdraw from office, business, or active life, usually because of age."[2] Think about that sentence. Withdrawing from an active life because of age. That doesn't define me just yet. If that's your goal, that's not where I plan to take you during the course of this book.

As the time to hang up my suits and ties approached, I worked with my law firm to create a plan that allowed me to reduce my time in the office. I did not quit but worked to make myself more efficient and essential while working remotely. This allowed Patty and I to spend more time on the road. This was our plan.

Are you thinking about a strategy that doesn't include having the fire department wheel you past your support staff? Are you willing to invest some of your time and allocate resources to get there? If you are thinking about a strategy whereby you have a goal and are committed to it, read on. I think you will find some ideas to help you arrive at the landing zone that you have identified.

Your Future Is Lurking in Your Past

Some of the stories I'm sharing with you are from my childhood and young adulthood. I picked up some important skills and knowledge during these phases of my life, most often inadvertently. What I learned from the start provided a foundation upon which to build. These lessons, coupled with a few good habits I acquired, would serve me throughout my lifetime.

In later chapters, I'll relay how my circuitous career in law led to experience in practically all forms of legal organizations. I served in the public sector before joining the ranks of lawyers in private practice. I have been a solo practitioner, an associate in a small firm, a partner, and of counsel in a small law firm, a large law firm, and a very large law firm. I was once a law clerk. I helped build a small law firm and have been part of the management team in a big firm. I graduated to working part-time, mentoring younger lawyers and helping them build their practices. I tried my last case and recorded my last billable hour. I'm no longer a working lawyer. And I'm not retired. I've much left to accomplish.

---

[2] *Random House Unabridged Dictionary of American English,* (2022), s.v. "to retire."

What about my life will make any difference to you in planning your future? We all have a story, each different and interesting. Once you get beyond the uniqueness of genetic composition, there are similarities in the background of most professionals. Not one of us started in first place.

Lurking in our pasts are learning experiences that have been stacked upon each other. Piece-by-piece, morsels from our lives were bound together to create who we've become. The meandering path I took was full of interesting people, mentors, and a few rogues. Your path likely included a similar cast of characters. By reading about people and events that influenced me, something may click. Maybe you'll think:

"I had a similar thing happen to me."

"That's a meaningful person in my life I haven't stopped to think about in a long time."

"What fun we had. We should do it again."

What does looking back have to do with helping you going forward? Perhaps it will put in motion a thought process by which you contemplate what made you tick when you were in law school, as a youngish attorney, a new parent, an aspiring soccer coach, or vacationing beach-goer. Share those bits of your story with yourself and perhaps a loved one. Take some time and think about it. Your past can be your teacher.

When I reflected on my experiences, I realized that there were many personal accomplishments. They were interspersed with a good number of difficulties. Every problem offered me an opportunity to overcome the challenge it presented. My personal stories will, I hope, inspire you to take a glance at your own life and career.

I also included stories of people from other walks of life and professions to provide inspiration as you begin your journey. They are ordinary people who have accomplished extraordinary things.

Take a few moments to do the simple exercises and build upon each of them to help you to determine your next steps. Looking back at the road you traveled will help you plot a smoother route forward.

There was no one event, single conversation, or middle-of-the-night revelation that led me to this moment in my life. Some days were a slog. The days turned into months, then months into years. Somehow, I ended up at the point where I was in command of my career and my future. And now, here I am typing these words from an apartment in the

South of France: a place Patty and I wished to one day be since I was 19 years old.

It's Like Planning a Trip

We've always found planning for a vacation or weekend trip to be an enjoyable part of our travels. We learned about a destination new to us. Sometimes we took time to pick up basic phrases needed to get by in a foreign country: "Hello and goodbye," "please and thank you," and most importantly, "Where are the bathrooms?" When we arrived in Krakow, or Istanbul, we sounded polite. Our poor accents and limited vocabulary quickly betrayed us, and our hosts responded in English. They appreciated the effort and often complimented us on trying to speak a bit of the local language.

Your journey through these pages is akin to planning a trip. Some of it you know, but you will also learn new things along the way. Sure, there are some elements to the process that will be tedious. It's the same as getting beyond simple phrases in a language you don't speak. But that's okay. This trip will be a pleasure because of what it yields. Like anything else you've chosen to pursue, the reward, in the end, will be worth it to you. I encourage you to spend the same amount of energy as you do planning a vacation in charting out the next phase of your career.

We all have our own dreams and goals. What you aspire to achieve will not be for me, and vice versa. My desire is to inspire you to enjoy a planning experience. By that, I don't mean for you to land where I have landed. What I was shooting for will be totally different than where you are aiming. I hope to get you moving toward *your* personal goals by helping you get off to a better start: my objective is for you to do it better than I was able to do.

People searching for change are generally looking for the same thing. We have different reasons for engaging in the search. Some never begin looking, content to let life take them along—which is fine. Others wish to be more deliberate in making what comes next come to life. When you have finished reading, I hope that you have a vision of the path to your future and that you know the general direction in which you are headed. It would be great if, during the time you are reading these words, you could take the first steps toward achieving your goals. That is, you begin to do what it takes to get there. Finally, and perhaps more complex, you appreciate why you are headed in that direction.

HOW ARE YOU? I'M BUSY.

"If you want to identify me, ask me not where I live, or what I like to eat, or how I comb my hair, but ask me what I am living for, in detail, ask me what I think is keeping me from living fully for the thing I want to live for."

–Thomas Merton, Trappist monk (1915–1968)[3]

"Hey man, I haven't seen you in forever. How've you been?"

"Busy, how about you?"

"I'm swamped."

This is a standard greeting. The opening question dares—no, begs—for the follow-up opportunity to declare we have not found enough hours in the day. How many times have you, or anybody with whom you opened your conversation in a similar fashion, and said, "Things are slow" or "I am really enjoying things; life is at a good pace"? What kind of response is "I'm busy," really? Why do we use it? I have, and I am guessing many, if not most of you, have as well. It's a bizarre custom.

I can only answer for myself as to why I responded to anyone who asked me how I was doing: overwhelmed by work and family obligations, stressed, or just trying to impress.

How are you doing? How about "I'm broke" or "I'm waiting for the phone to ring as my practice is floundering"—not likely to happen. What if we shucked the routine answer to the welcoming "how are you?" in exchange for: "My dog ran off, and the truck broke down, but I'm okay" or "Great, tremendous"?

I've thought about fashioning a response more along the lines of the Christmas letters we send and receive just to see the reaction. "I'm doing great, got a raise, moved to a bigger home, traded the Benz for a Jag, Susie's making straight As, and Johnny was paroled in the fall."

---

[3] Martin, James, Robert Ellsberg, Daniel P. Horan, and Kaya Oakes. *What I Am Living For: Lessons from the Life and Writings of Thomas Merton.* Edited by Jon M. Sweeney. Notre Dame, IN: Ave Maria Press, 2018.

Some years ago, when our children were teenagers, I discovered that they really did listen. Not to my periodic lectures or pontifications, but to my more routine phrases. I was informed that shortly before every family trip, old dad would reach a point where I would profess, "I don't know how I am ever going to be ready. I'm not sure I can go." I assure you, I was not stressed about cutting the grass.

Our kids, who, no doubt staged the moment, called me out on my use of this pet phrase. They asked Patty in my presence, "Has he said it yet, Mom?" Upon hearing their memory of how the family vacations started, I dropped the phrase. I was often reminded of my old habit and am subjected to good-natured ridicule whenever hauling the suitcases up from the basement. Our 38-year-old son, also a lawyer, confessed to having incorporated this phrase into his vacation-packing repertoire.

This habit—or obsession—of describing ourselves as "busy" to any available ear is not unique to lawyers. The badge of being busy appears to be worn by those from various walks of life. When discussing this topic with a friend, a nun from a local Catholic college, she told me of a quote hanging over her desk. It was a reminder to her of the downside of being too busy. Sister Norma shared the words from her wall, penned by Thomas Merton: "The frenzy of the activist (that's us) . . . destroys the fruitfulness of one's own work because it kills the root of inner wisdom which makes work fruitful." I have not read any of Merton's books but have promised to pick one up—when I'm not too busy.

In search of the opposite of busy, the pace of life in France comes to mind. People there enjoy *un café* (coffee) in a café, not in a Styrofoam cup while walking down the street. "*Ça va*?" (How are you?) is responded to with "*Ça va bien.*" (it's going well, or I'm doing well), or "*Impeccable*" (impeccable, perfect, flawless), not "I am busy."

The French know how to not be busy. In general, they simply enjoy life. Not just because some have a 35-hour work week, 5 weeks of vacation, plus every holiday known to man, and then some. When's the last time your shop closed for Whit Monday (also known as Pentecost Monday, or Monday of the Holy Spirit)? It would be a day off if you were working in France. In many cities and towns, life moves at the pace of a two-hour lunch.

While on vacation with our kids, we had dinner in France in a restaurant on July 14—the day France celebrates its national holiday, la Fête nationale français, this is Bastille Day to Americans. The place was on a beach and overflowing with patrons. It was a great celebration. There was dancing and fireworks over the Mediterranean. I looked down the beach and noticed that almost all the other restaurants, each with the same great view of the sea, were closed. I asked a young waitress why the other restaurants were closed, missing the opportunity for a full house on a festive night. She responded that the owners of the other restaurants worked to live. Her boss lived to work, dragging her along with him on a national holiday.

The French have incorporated into their vocabulary the Italian word for not being busy—*farniente*, which means idleness or doing nothing. According to authors Ira and Barbara Spector, it connotes a state of "peace, tranquility, and bliss."[4]

My father's routine response to 'How are you doing today?' was "I'm doing the best I can." One of these, or some variation, may launch an interesting conversation, but not about work. Perhaps we cannot break this habit of professing busyness to all who will listen. Yet, a break in the action for a little *farniente* is always a remedy for a frenetic pace, even if temporary. How can you say you are busy if you are lying on a beach? Merton and others may be worth a read to find a snippet of advice on the topic. Of course, this requires us to neglect the cell phone for a bit, a topic for another day. I need to wind this bit up. I'm busy.

[4] Spector, Ira and Barbara Spector. *A Month of Sundays: Villa Life in the South of France.* Arius Publications, 2003.

Exercise #1

How Busy Am I?

---

a. Name three things you missed because you were too busy:

b. Identify three people you disappointed because you were too busy:

PART I

Connect the Dots

> "You can't connect the dots looking forward; you can only connect them looking backwards."[1]
>
> —Steve Jobs, American business magnate (1955–2011)

Writer and philosopher George Santayana wrote, "Those who cannot remember the past are condemned to repeat it."[2] You've seen this concept expressed in various iterations of Santayana's quote. It's been borrowed and modified by many along the way. As it pertains to why people go to war or how they mismanage a country, this idea has some application. But repeating part of your past may be exactly what you need to do. I'm referring to repeating what got you to where you sit today. In Bob Marley's words, "In this bright future, you can't forget your past."[3] Why do I believe this to be true?

---

1 Jobs, Steve. "2005 Stanford Commencement Address." June 12, 2005. Video. https://youtu.be/UF8uR6Z6KLc.

2 Santayana, George. "The life of Reason: Five Volumes in One." Echo Library, 2006. https://www.goodreads.com/work/quotes/392659-the-life-of-reason-or-the-phases-of-human-progress-a-selection-of-essa.

3 BrainyQuote. "Bob Marley Quotes." Accessed April 12, 2023. https://www.brainyquote.com/quotes/bob_marley_377817.

You've been successful in your life by building on what you know. During the course of your career, you've pursued things you enjoy. You've put to work the talents you possess to achieve your niche on this planet. This section is about looking back on *that* past and building on it, repeating what has worked for you—connecting the dots of your successes, talents, and interests to lead you in the direction you choose.

1

See Your Future, Don't Wander into It

WHO CARES? YOU DO, AND THAT'S WHAT MATTERS!

> "They always say time changes things, but you actually have to change them yourself."[1]
>
> —Andy Warhol, American artist (1928–1987)

In 1969, the group *Chicago* released the song "Does Anybody Really Know What Time It Is?"[2] I was 16 when I first heard this music. More recently, a twist on the song whispered in my head as I was doodling, planning what to write about lawyers' retirements and changes of pace or switching careers.

Looking around the law firm as I was contemplating a change, I asked myself, "Does anybody here really care about what I did in my life?" Should I have died in the saddle, it's certain that my memory would have been evoked shortly after I permanently stopped coming to the office. My former colleagues would have complained loudly about what a collector I was during my 40 years of being a lawyer. They would gripe as they cleaned out my desk and pulled the artwork, awards, and diplomas from the walls.

At the end of the day, will anyone notice what you achieved in your professional life? What mark did you leave on the world, your business, and your profession? Did you change the world, leave a legacy, or contribute to some greater body of work? Did you leave words by which to live

---

1 Warhol, Andy. "Time." In *The Philosophy of Andy Warhol (From A to B & Back Again)*. Harcourt Brace Jovanovich, 1975.

2 Chicago. "Does Anybody Really Know What Time It Is?" Recorded January 1969. Track 2 side one on *Chicago Transit Authority*. Columbia, 1969, LP record.

that others will turn to for generations? When the after-funeral reception is over and friends have returned to their offices, how fast will you fade from their conversations?

By the time the bronze nameplate next to my old office door is replaced to identify the next dweller, I suspect folks will have moved on. I decided not to allow this scene to be my inelegant farewell to the firm, even though it may have been accompanied by another great tune, "Don't get around much anymore."[3] But where to begin?

TIME IS NOT AN ABUNDANT COMMODITY

I urge you to devote some of your immediate attention to thinking about the next steps, making tweaks or dramatic changes in your life, or retirement if that is your desire. As I worked on this book I was saddened by the accounts shared with me by lawyers lamenting that time got away from them because their lives were shaped by their work.

As you turn these pages, you are getting older. Only by minutes of course. But those minutes turn to hours, days, weeks, months, and so on. You will not regret adding a sense of urgency to getting started.

However, you will very much regret it if one day you look back thinking: "If only I'd taken that camel ride in the Sahara when I had the physical ability to do so;" "I wish I had the health to take a canoe ride down the river or a bike ride along the tow path;" or "We should have taken that cruise with the kids. Why did I think I had no time for vacations?" Those days are not recoverable—look forward.

At the celebration of life for my 58-year-old brother-in-law, Mike, I chatted with his fraternity brothers, golf buddies, and his family. They came from all over the country to celebrate the life of their brother, friend, and colleague. He touched many people during his time here on Earth, as evidenced by the large group gathered to see him off. I talked to a lot of people at the funeral and gatherings associated with it. One of the conversations I had stuck with me.

Mourning the loss of his long-time pal, one of Mike's good friends, a lawyer I know, expressed to me the unfairness of this good guy being felled by cancer at such a young age. We commiserated observing the

---

[3] Russell, Bob, lyricist. 1942. "Don't Get Round Much Anymore." By Duke Ellington and his Famous Orchestra. Recorded May 4, 1940. Robbins Music.

obvious: how we'd miss his humor, great smile, and Mike's unique flair when expressing disappointment with something—or someone. Our talk drifted beyond musing over what being taken at age 58 meant. Mike would miss his sons' weddings, retiring with my sister to travel and play golf, teasing grandchildren, and just being here to enjoy more golf and good times with family and friends.

Mike's lawyer friend steered our wistful conversation into a reflection on his own life. The guy is a healthy, 58-year-old successful attorney. He and his wife have young adult children. His interests go beyond the law, but he is "busy." We talked about what he liked to do outside the office, dwelling on how difficult it is to find the time to fully pursue these other passions. Trials and all that goes with them interfere with his ability to spend more time traveling and enjoying life.

The funeral provoked him to ponder, and express out loud, that he better start reading the tea leaves as they relate to his own life. As we shook hands and parted, Mike's friend left me with "I need to get the message."

Contemplating what is important in one's own life is a common reflection when standing at the funeral of a family member or a dear friend. What rattles through your head may be unsettling if you are the same age as the deceased.

Take the time to plan to do what you most enjoy now. You can't do it all at once. But there should be an urgency to getting started. Don't wait for a funeral for your inspiration. Time is not an abundant commodity.

HOW WILL YOU BE REMEMBERED?

"How do you want to be remembered?" This is probably not the first time you've heard the question. It's worth taking a moment to think about your answer. If you're like me, you've put it off for any number of seemingly valid reasons, especially with "I'm busy." This is probably one of the most popular phrases in the lawyer's arsenal. It works for nearly every occasion.

- Perhaps you think you're too far from the day when you empty your briefcase—or backpack—and toss it on the closet floor for the last time. Fair enough. You may be entirely satisfied, driven, and not in for a change until you're handed your 50-year recognition pin.
- Perhaps you're of a mind that you're too far down the road and too old to switch gears. But, maybe, there is another fork in the career road or the path of life for you to explore. You may stumble upon it. You may

actively seek it. In any event, you owe it to yourself to be prepared to manage the decision you must make when you hit that moment.

Stop everything right now and think about the end of your life, just for a moment. It will help put everything from your past, present, and future into perspective.

My friend Jim's tombstone expresses in bold letters who he was in life. FATHER, FRIEND, ADVOCATE. He loved the mountains at Breckenridge, Colorado, and a silhouette of the Rocky Mountains adorns the marker.

Jim was a tenacious litigator, represented by a shark circling on his headstone. He loved these images. Jim was also mischievous, constantly joking and pulling pranks, a legacy that is inscribed on his marker:

When my days are over
And my time has come to pass
Please bury me upside down
So the world may kiss my ass.

NOW IT'S YOUR TURN

Jot down what may be your first thoughts on how your commemorative inscription will read. This is not a morbid task. Why let your kids, friends, or surviving family members define you after your departure? You need to have a say.

If you have a poetic streak in you, a clever inscription may bring more visitors. Here are a few to inspire your creative juices:

Here lays Butch,
we planted him raw.
He was quick on the
trigger, but slow on the
draw.

No secret how this fellow met his maker. Butch resides permanently in Silver City, Nevada.

This one is from Battersea, London. It's not flattering. The quip tells us more than the deceased probably would have liked for all to know. He let his creditors define him for eternity:

Owen Moore
Gone away

Owin' more
Than he could pay.

A few words are fine. I jotted down a few examples of brief thoughts to share with your future visitors to get you started. Be creative. Be honest. Be yourself.

Here rests one happy, crazy lawyer.
I billed 3,000 hours in my last year of practice.
I could have hit 3,500 but I'm here.
Loved by the kids, favored by the dog.

Here's a headstone poem I penned that I hope you don't use. If you do, I'll know that you didn't finish reading this book.

I've missed my billable hours' goal
Please, dear Lord, will you save my soul?
For it was you who summoned me while in court
Thus rendering my argument five minutes short.

Exercise #1

Write Your Epitaph

Stop for a few moments to think about how you would like to be remembered. Take a piece of paper or open up a blank document on your computer screen. Jot down one or two sentences. You don't need to be expansive, dramatic, or poetic unless you wish. This is just for you—no need to share it with anyone unless you're so inspired. If you really like your work, put it with your estate plan for future use. You can still have a say even after your final day.

THINKING ABOUT A DIFFERENT DIRECTION

I mentioned that I employed a career coach. At the time, my firm allotted a small stipend for partners to use toward professional development. This was a thoughtful perk. I coupled what the law firm allocated with my own funds. It was a solid investment in myself. Here is how I decided to seek help from someone with the proper skills to give me direction.

In 2006, I was 52 years old. That year, I represented a man accused of murder in a two-week jury trial. It ended in a hung jury. It was the third time I had tried the case. The first trial ended in a hung jury. My client's conviction in the second trial was reversed on appeal. It was stressful and exhausting. Just before the third trial, my law partner and I merged our 10-person law firm into an operation of about 100 lawyers. There were billable-hour requirements and high expectations of me in our new environment. I was also preparing to serve as the president of the Indianapolis Bar Association. Our family was busy with school and sports. To add to matters, that year my younger brother Terry died after an 18-month battle with cancer. He was only 50 years of age. I worked almost every day and felt as though I was chasing my tail. I was on the verge of exhaustion.

My life had four components at that time. There was work and all things associated with it. This accounted for most of my time. There is no reason to expand upon this segment of how I was spending that time. This one, you understand.

Then there was family. There are several family activities and traditions that I cherish. Rarely did I permit the tether of a law practice to keep me from enjoying them. All three of our kids, Sean, Maureen, and Colleen, were involved in sports. It was great fun following them through soccer, gymnastics, volleyball, and every sport a Catholic grade school offered. I didn't miss many games, matches, or meets. For several years I went to the school once a month and introduced 5th-graders to travel and the French language. As coach of the St. Pius X track team, I left the office early two days a week in the spring for some years. Managing 80 grade-school athletes took a few hours of weekend time during track season. Patty and I enjoyed this time of our lives. Of course, the time spent away from the office had to be made up, but I did have some personal priorities.

There has been a gathering at our house for Sunday night dinner for more than 30 years. We started this tradition when our children were young.

It continues to this day. Sunday night was shared with our kids. When they were still with us, our parents were there too. As our children were growing up, they shared time with their grandparents almost every week. Sometimes our siblings and their children would eat with us. We have several good friends who joined us at times. There could be anywhere from 8 to 20 people around the table on Sunday evenings. That ritual is still sacred and practiced every Sunday when we are in Indianapolis.

Travel was the third facet of my life at the time. I didn't have many entire weekends off, so time away from work usually involved a trip. Patty and I managed a few excursions every year, some with our children and others on our own.

Preparation for time away from my law practice involved expending tremendous energy to leave my cases in a reasonable state. The result was that many vacations started with me being thoroughly exhausted. I started two ski trips so wiped out that on the first day out of the office—while the others skied—I slept in the backseat of a rental car. I can tell you that the parking garages at the slopes are not heated. I couldn't muster the energy to get out of the car, let alone put on a pair of ski boots to attack the mountain.

It seemed that time away from the office was not worth the toll. There were always emergencies waiting at the end of however long I had gone despite my toil before I left. Many of my colleagues have shared with me the sentiment that leaving the office for more than a few days was never worth the pain. The stress of preparing for a vacation and the strain I felt upon returning from time away seemed to undo the fun of my time off.

The fourth category of my life at that time I would describe as everything else. Spotty pleasure reading, limited work around the house, and socializing with friends some weekends. I exercised sporadically and engaged in no hobbies unless I counted the infrequent reading. I also studied French on and off for many years to enhance the experience of our travels to France.

I don't want to suggest that my life was a miserable existence; it was far from it. That's not the takeaway here. I enjoyed what I was doing most days. We had a lot of fun. Our kids were healthy, doing well in school, and caused us minimal heartburn as they grew into young adults. But I felt that I was missing something.

Also, I knew that the pace was unsustainable and unhealthy.

Unfortunately, it took me years to break this cycle. The version of me during that time of my life was consumed by work. I was blind to the need to recalibrate, get more efficient, and engage in more enjoyable and healthier, activities. I wrongly believed that doing so would take the time that I just did not have.

THE BEGINNINGS OF A PLAN

During the time I worked with my career coach, he asked that I compile a list of as many things as I could think of that I would like to do. The push I got from Mark was a game changer for me. I was instructed to allow no boundaries. I still have my checklist, which you will find at the back of this book in Appendix A. I listed my personal and professional goals, as well as the fun things I wanted to do. Some were short-term objectives, while others were going to take some time to accomplish. A few pipe dreams also made the inventory. The list of 38 things to do before I am infirm include:

- Get more exercise
- Find our relatives in Romania
- Continue to improve my French
- Learn Spanish
- Free up weekends from work
- Hone my legal practice to one area of law

It was a great exercise. I look at it today, 15 years later, to discover I haven't achieved some of the items on my list. I still have not learned to play the guitar or sailed the Caribbean. I can't speak German and I am not going to plant a garden to weed. But there's still time, and I am not giving up. I have greatly improved my French language skills, picked up some Spanish, and written a book. I also found a way to gracefully exit the practice of law.

Out of the 38 goals I wrote down in 2007, 21 have been accomplished so far.

It was a confluence of events that provoked me to begin to think about how to get off the treadmill and move in a different direction. It didn't happen overnight.

DO A LITTLE SPADE WORK

At the end of World War II, my dad came home after serving with the United States Marine Corps in the South Pacific. He was 22 years old. His father was an Irish immigrant with little education. My grandfather, Patrick McGough, arrived in the United States from County Monahan, Ireland, in 1902. He brought with him two silver dollars and an eighth-grade education. He dug ditches, laid bricks, and drove a truck in Cleveland, Ohio. He raised two children as well. My father was three years old when his mother died shortly after the birth of my aunt Mary.

My dad, like most young veterans, needed work. The story goes that my grandfather, Paddy, took my dad to work with him one day at the cemetery where he was then working. He handed my dad a shovel and told him to dig a grave while Paddy watched. Dad never finished. Three-quarters of the way through the arduous task, he jumped out of the unfinished hole in the ground. He told my grandfather that he had decided to use the Veteran's Administration benefits he had earned and would enroll in college at John Carroll University. My dad had done all of the spade work he needed, literally and figuratively, to convince himself that he had no desire to follow in the professional footsteps of his father. Off he went to college.

None of us are going to have to dig a hole in the ground as part of our plan, but research is vital to your success. The spade work of reading and consulting with people who have the expertise and who you trust will pay dividends.

Throughout my personal inquiry, I used every means I could find. We found a great resource in our financial planner and I did research online on every topic from saving for retirement to where we should live.

As I mentioned earlier, I would visit the aisle mislabeled "self-help" in various bookstores. It was there that I discovered Victor Frankl's *Man's Search for Meaning* and *The Alchemist* by Paulo Coelho, residing near *The Relationship Rescue Workbook* penned by Dr. Phil. It's not all about personal failings in the land of self-help. Maybe there's a better label for this section in bookshops.

Dad would have approved of my spade work. I was asking questions of people with the proper expertise, doing my research and gaining information as I began my formal quest to examine what was next for me. Your spade work will be critical to your success. It's perhaps the most important part of the program. Educating yourself will help guide you to your answers and your goals. There is just no substitute for rolling up your shirtsleeves and digging in.

IDENTIFYING GOALS

Here are some ideas for professional goals to get you started. Do you want to:

- Be the best lawyer in your field in the city, state, in the entire US?
- Retire from the law at age 50 and teach school for 15 years?
- Go in-house with a company?
- Grow your solo or small firm practice to 5, 10, or 20 lawyers?
- Move to somewhere warm and start a bed-and-breakfast?

Personal goals are just that—personal. Everyone will have a unique list. These are goals personal to you.

Maybe you want to run a marathon; learn to speak Polish; bike through Italy; quit working on weekends; or coach your kid's soccer team.

This is the easy part. Before getting down to the real work, give some thought to what obstacles you will encounter when you set out and try to make some headway. What gremlins await to frustrate your progress? If you search for them at the outset, you'll be better prepared to combat the distractions that may keep you from achieving your desired development.

Let me share the list I made to give you a few ideas:

- Fear of failure
- Family commitments
- Work commitments
- Lack of discipline/organization
- Procrastination
- Money

There may be some common denominators between your obstacles list and mine. This checklist is not exhaustive, and the points I identified when I was sorting through a similar exercise are fairly obvious. Some of these will not apply, and you will likely have other potential obstacles that I either didn't have or didn't envision.

Exercise #2
Identifying Goals:

---

1. List 10 things you want to accomplish in your life.

2. Identify the 3 things you could start to work on in the next 12 months.

3. Highlight one of the objectives that you can start working on today.

Exercise #3

Distractions and Obstacles:

Write down three snags that might interfere with your progress:

1.

2.

3.

You will rarely be bored if you continually look down the road. It's important to enjoy the challenges, rewards, and good days of your current stage of life's path. But you won't remain in this moment for long. Savor it but be thinking about where you wish to go, short-term and long-term.

Begin your spade work. Gather information and educate yourself. There's no shortage of resources for you to tap. Perhaps you'll want to acquire new skills that will serve you in your next stage. It may not be seamless. There'll be a few bumps.

Don't attempt to put your plan together overnight. Arm yourself with information, and then take time to reflect on your talents and interests. Identify the perceived obstacles that may interfere with your progress, such as issues of funding, inability to make the time commitment, and plain old procrastination. Like any problem you face in your law practice, there is a work-around for every barrier. Some options are easier to achieve, others more palatable. Once committed to looking forward, if you work at it, you will surprise yourself with your progress.

CAREER INSPIRATION: CHEF DAVID YATES

David Yates was born in the London suburb of Kent in the early days of World War II. The bombs the Germans were dropping on the city were fireworks to the lad. He watched the fiery bursts from a tree he had scaled to get a better view until his grannie would pull him to the safety of the family's backyard bomb shelter.

Though the war ended in 1945, many deprivations continued in England. Basic foodstuffs were still being rationed, a practice that did not end until 1954. Clothing, soap, petrol, and even bread were on ration well after the war was over.

The England in which David came of age was a bit of a tough place to grow up during the decade or so after the end of the war. A trip to the neighborhood shops in London took David and his pals past bomb craters that marked lots where houses once stood, where people once lived, and where some died during the Blitz.

David's father worked in a factory making turbines for large machines. He arrived at the house after work in the evening, his clothing covered in the grime from his day on the job. He stopped in the garage to dip his hands in a tin of goo designed to remove the grease before sitting down to dinner.

At age 15, David was looking for a bit of direction. Under the British education system, he needed to select a path at age 16: university, trade school, or just go to work. He was in school but not particularly interested in the university route.

When asked what career path he planned to pursue, David responded that he did not know. His dad offered to set David up with a job working alongside him in the factory. David would not need to invest much energy in the effort. His father would speak to the folks doing the hiring, and David would have a job.

Many men throughout England during the post-war period held these types of jobs as industry came back to life. The pay from a factory job would put food on the table and a roof over one's head. Tough work done by tough men. It would have been an easy decision for David—let his dad line up a job for him, grab his lunch pail, and trot off to make parts for turbines every working day for the next 30 years. After observing his father and other men in the neighborhood trudge back home after a day at the factory, David wasn't too keen on following that career path. He was certain of that. He knew what he didn't want to do. But what did he want to do?

In the 1950s, the British Broadcasting Corporation (BBC) aired the television program *Eagle Magazine* twice a week. The host introduced British kids to venues far beyond their neighborhoods, such as the Alps, Africa, and America. The program also showcased different trades. One week an electrician, the next perhaps a plumber would demonstrate how they worked and what they did at their jobs. The program enthralled David. He tried not to miss an episode. It led him to understand that the world was larger than his corner of Kent. There were jobs other than in the factory with his dad, but until *Eagle Magazine*, he had not been exposed to them.

To this day, David still recalls watching a cook vigorously attack an onion with his knife as he described his profession to the viewers of *Eagle Magazine*. As the chef quickly sliced the veggie with incredible speed and precision, he explained that a chef could work anywhere in the world. There was no foreign language requirement. The trade of being a chef was totally transportable. David perked up. At that moment, sitting before the family television in Kent, David decided, "That's what I'm going to do. I want to be a chef."

David and his parents acted on his enthusiasm. His mom and dad helped him enroll in the best culinary school in London, where he studied for two years. David's first job was in the kitchen at what was then the largest hotel in London. As the television chef promised, David's cooking skills worked beyond the shores of Britain. Before long, he was off to France, where his abilities were honed in the kitchen at Le Laurent, a Michelin-starred restaurant in Paris.

Back in England after his stint in France, David lived and worked in London in the 1960s. Sean Connery occasionally popped in to eat pasta at the staff table in the kitchen at the White Elephant Club, where David was a chef. Famous British rock-and-roll stars, actors, and royalty frequented the several clubs he worked in during that period. It was hard work and an exciting life for a young man.

Over the course of his career, David cooked in the kitchen of the ocean liner RMS Queen Mary, in restaurants across the United States, Europe, and on several islands in the Caribbean. David moved through the ranks over the years. He ultimately set aside his apron and toque, left the kitchen, and served as general manager for several large enterprises, opening 36 restaurants throughout the world.

A television program planted the seed in a 15-year-old that bloomed into an interesting and successful career spanning several continents. David is now retired in the South of France, enjoying a good life with his wife, Debbie. He's a short flight back to Kent but a long way from the couch where *Eagle Magazine* inspired David to act.

2

To Know Where You're Going, Know Where You've Been

HUMBLE BEGINNINGS

> "Odd things happen to all of us on our way through life without our noticing for a time that they ever happened."[1]
>
> —*Peter Pan,* J.M. Barrie, Scottish novelist and playwright (1860–1937)

Where you have been will greatly impact where you are going. The influences of people and experiences you've encountered along the way have directed you to where you've been through the various segments of your life. A serious inquiry into who you want to be, personally and professionally, what you're after, and where you want to end up should include a reflection on your past.

This is not something we tend to spend much time on when focused on our working lives. First, it takes years of focus and hard work to achieve the level of competence required to be a good lawyer. It doesn't happen overnight. Though I don't know that it's for the best, it's normal that one isn't focused on the long-term future during the first 5 or 10 years in the game. You could argue that it makes no sense to strive to succeed in this business while at the same time trying to figure out what else you are looking for. Then again, maybe you wish to practice law forever. If not, why not give at least a passing thought to where your career path is leading before you hit 60?

We spend too little time thinking about ourselves because we've convinced ourselves that we're too busy. Setting aside time in our schedules

[1] Barrie, J. M. *Peter Pan.* Puffin, 2014.

for some serious self-reflection may look ridiculous next to our list of appointments with important clients, our trial schedules, and deal closings: "I can't waste time on thinking about my future. I'm too busy." At least, that was my thought process during much of my career.

WHO HAS YOUR BACK? A LESSON FROM DAD ON GETTING PAID FOR MY WORK

I was the beneficiary of much useful advice throughout my life, frequently offered by unpaid advisors. My father was there to help me out through a thorny issue I encountered during my first paying job. I was having difficulty collecting from a customer on my paper route.

My first big break came at age 10. My friend Jimmy went on vacation and entrusted me to his *Indianapolis Times* paper route. This led to me securing my own paper route, my first step toward financial independence. During my first year in business in 1963, I sold enough subscriptions to win a trip to Washington D.C. It was my first travel odyssey.

Shepherding two busloads of paper carriers around the nation's capital meant *The Times* had a set program for us. I nonetheless attempted to schedule myself into the White House. I wrote President John F. Kennedy to announce my visit. Kenneth O'Donnell, his appointments secretary, wrote back. He let me down gently, telling me that the President would be out of town the weekend of my scheduled visit. He would not be able to meet with me. I went on the trip anyway.

It was my first time on a carrier bus and my initial trip away from my parents. Though I was a fifth-grader, I was assigned to share my first hotel room with two eighth-graders. I abused my parents' trust by jumping on the bed, trying to touch the ceiling. My older and more sophisticated roommates defied authority by smoking a pack of cigarettes in the hotel room.

A LESSON FROM DAD ON GETTING PAID

Paperboys (and papergirls as there were a few at the time) were entrepreneurs. We collected the cost of the paper from each customer on our route once a week. On Saturday mornings, we met our manager, Mr. Pressman, in the parking lot of Jordan's Drug Store. There we paid for the papers we delivered from the funds we had collected. Our profit was what remained. Any outstanding funds not collected cut into the paperboy's pocket, not the profit of *The Indianapolis Times*. We were thus motivated to "collect for the *Times*," the chant used when knocking on our customers' doors.

I had a serious drag on profitability one year. One of my customers was a single man who lived a street over from us. Mr. Creek was the ultimate slow pay. When a customer paid, they were given a receipt in the form of a small ticket torn from the page of a book. It was dated and marked "Paid," denoting the week for which they had paid for the paper. Mr. Creek had very few of these receipts in his possession. That is because they still resided in my book. Page after page of his unpaid tickets. I was 11 years old, carrying my customer's debt.

My friend Jimmy had schooled me in the art of collecting. It was best to appear at a customer's house around dinner time on Friday evening. Many people picked up their paychecks on Friday. Arriving at their front door to collect when they were flush with cash was an early lesson in timing "the ask."

However, Mr. Creek professed to never have cash—not on Friday, not on Saturday morning, not on any other day of the week when I caught him at home. He was rarely there. Sometimes he wouldn't answer the door when I showed up. His bill was mounting, and the way the system worked, I was buying his paper for him. I hatched a plan to surprise Mr. Creek and collect what he owed.

THE CREEK AMBUSH OF 1964

My brother Terry and I were in the phase of playing army in the neighborhood. We owned all the gear.

We had World War II army surplus store fatigue jackets that were way too big for us. We had helmets, my dad's canteen from his Marine Corps service, medals for valor, toy guns, the whole bit. One weekday morning, I got up before 6:00 a.m. and pulled on my fatigue jacket, filled my canteen, and grabbed my helmet and collection book. It was my best Green Beret look. I lacked only the camouflage face paint. Mom banned the use of camo paint after it was applied to a younger brother against his wishes. I headed out in the dark to ambush Mr. Creek as he went to his car to go to work.

I arrived at the battleground before dawn. There were lights on in the house. My target was still home. I positioned myself deep inside the branches of a forsythia bush near the sidewalk. I waited, staying still, poised to execute an ambush like the soldiers in the movies Dad took us to watch on the occasional Saturday afternoon.

When Mr. Creek walked out his front door, he was confronted by an 11-year-old commando. Armed with my collection book, I leaped from the forsythia, initiating my predawn surprise attack. Hollering "Collect for the *Times*," I charged into the breech, forsythia branches hung from the camouflage net on the steel helmet that bounced over my eyes with every step as I ran toward the enemy. Now I had Mr. Creek! I surprised the hell out of him.

Despite the precision of my planning and flawless execution, I didn't get paid. Mr. Creek performed his well-practiced pocket shuffle. It was the same act he had perfected on me during daylight hours. He patted here and there. He turned the pockets on his trousers inside out. He opened his wallet to show me it was empty. He thoroughly frisked himself in the dark but turned up nothing. Not a dime. Once again, I came up empty. Dejected, I retreated to base camp, our house on Durham Drive, to get ready for school.

THE COUNTER ATTACK

When I got home, Dad had not yet left for work. As he ate his Rice Krispies cereal, I shared with him the details of my failed ambush. He knew of my struggle with getting Mr. Creek to pay for his newspaper. It had been the topic of conversation at the family dinner table. He had left me to my own devices in my effort to get paid. Mom and Dad often allowed us to sort things out on our own, stepping in when they felt the timing was right. As Dad and I strategized over our breakfast cereals, it became clear that the failure of my predawn collection effort was the last straw for Dad. He told me he would now help me collect from Mr. Creek.

I'LL FIX YOUR WAGON

Without offering any detail, Dad said he would "fix his wagon." Though he had no way of knowing, this was ominous for Mr. Creek. When Pop threatened to fix your wagon, what followed was never good. The phrase was only trotted out when a transgression needed a response via some form of discipline. As children, Dad routinely fixed our wagons as part of our upbringing. In cases of serious transgressions our wagons were fixed by Dad, resorting to his Marine Corps training, announcing one was "confined to quarters" that is, grounded—forbidden to leave the premises. The wagon fixing was sometimes accomplished by a sentence to manual labor: painting the fence, weeding the rose bed, or, even worse, picking up Skippy's dog droppings in the backyard. Having Dad fix your wagon by being confined to quarters for a week was preferable to the latter. Seen from Dad's perspective, he was helping us mend our ways, but you never wanted Dad to fix your wagon. Mr. Creek was going to get it.

We waited until Friday evening and the prospect that Mr. Creek had been paid for whatever he'd been doing all week. Near dark, Dad went with me to collect. When we arrived at the Creek residence, I could see through a window that a party was going on. A couple of well-dressed women were sitting on the couch holding drinks and smoking cigarettes. The small living room was filled with people. At Dad's prompting, I banged on the door and shouted, "Collect for the *Times*." The party chatter stopped. Everyone was looking at me, standing there with my collection book full of their host's unpaid tickets. Mr. Creek came to the door. Before he could speak, Dad stepped up behind me and said loud enough for all the partygoers to hear: "You need to quit stiffing this kid. Pay him what you owe for the newspaper right now."

After many months, I'd finally caught Mr. Creek with money in his pocket. He pulled out a fat wallet in front of his guests. I've long forgotten the amount, 10 or 20 bucks. That's a lot when the paper cost about 75 cents a week. The next day, I told my manager that I had finally collected from this guy. As Pop suggested, I also told him that I would no longer deliver Mr. Creek's paper. I fired him as a customer. Mr. Creek paid me and within 24 hours had his newspaper cut off. Dad fixed *his* wagon.

BUILDING ON PERSONAL ACCOMPLISHMENTS: PAYING MY WAY THROUGH SCHOOL

While supervising the construction of the Jesuit high school in Indianapolis, where he would serve as its first president, Father William J. Schmidt, SJ, was living at our parish. Father Schmidt knew my father as he had been my dad's religion teacher at John Carroll University.

One Sunday, when I was in the eighth grade, my brother Terry and I were serving Mass for Father Schmidt. After Mass, he asked if we would like to attend the school he was starting, Brebeuf Preparatory School. I am the oldest of 6 kids. Terry was 15 months younger than me, a year behind me in school. We knew the Jesuit school would not be in the family budget and told Father Schmidt we would likely be attending our township school. He told us, "I want you to take the entrance exam. If you pass, I will make it happen."

I passed the entrance exam. Maybe every boy that took it passed that year. When Father Schmidt learned of this accomplishment, he visited our house. Priests didn't often come to our house; he was the first one I remember. Father Schmidt came with an appetite and a proposal for our family: he offered me a job at the school. I would put in 200 hours, and for each hour worked, $1.00 would be credited against the $400 tuition. My parents would have to cover the balance of my freshman year's fees.

I'm not certain how they could have said no. This was my father's former religion teacher and the first priest to be in our living room, offering Mom and Dad this fabulous deal in front of the whole family to allow their eldest to attend a Jesuit high school. How could they? It was a brilliant technique that Father Schmidt employed and it was not unique to our family. Many other students had the opportunity for a Jesuit education by working off part of the tuition thanks to Father Schmidt.

In the summer of 1967, I began hitchhiking to Brebeuf in the mornings to cut grass, clean out lockers, and otherwise help the maintenance men. I was part of a crew of four or five other students whose families had made similar bargains with Father Schmidt, who also cut the same deal with Mom and Dad for my brother Terry the next year. I'm forever grateful to him. Attending Brebeuf turned out to be a great experience.

It seems that looking back, there was no rhyme or reason for me to have taken the path I carved for myself. In talking with other lawyers and professionals, I am not certain there was much of a strategy compared to theirs. I get the sense that this is true for many of us.

It's impossible to say whether I arrived at my current life by design when my deliberate choices were tossed in with outside influences. People looked out for me. My father made sure my paper route client paid up. Father Schmidt gave me a job so that I could attend a Jesuit high school. Later, a boss did not promote me so that I would stay in school.

At some point in my what's-next journey, I stopped and took time from my busy life to reflect on my past. There are insights to be found through such an exercise, keys to doors opening as I planned my future. When I took the time to analyze it, the quote from *Peter Pan* resonated. Did I notice what was happening as it unfolded? Not really.

Looking back at your life, you can identify accomplishments you achieved with the help of others and some you managed on your own. Use these to give you direction in figuring out what you want to do next. There are hints in your past if you take some time to ponder your achievements.

Exercise #1

Who's Got Your Back:

Name three people in your life who have supported you through difficulties (parents, spouse, friends, advisers, bosses, teachers):

1.

2.

3.

It doesn't matter how well you have planned—or not planned—your career up to this moment. As J.M. Barrie suggested, things happen to us without our noticing that they ever happened. You've arrived at this point. You are here and need to begin planning your next chapter starting today. Be strategic.

Get to where you wish to be in a more efficient way than I was able to.

3

Reading Cues and Taking Risks

> "I don't believe in taking foolish chances, but nothing can be accomplished if we don't take any chances at all."[1]
>
> —Charles Lindbergh, American aviator (1902–1974)

RECOGNIZING ROAD SIGNS: ARE YOU MISSING IMPORTANT CUES?

There is an old joke about a man seeking the Lord's help as floodwaters begin to rise around his house. As the water flowed into his living room, a woman in a canoe paddles up to him. He pokes his head out the door. She asks him to jump into the canoe and be saved from the flood.

The man declines, telling her, "The Lord will provide."

Next, as he hangs out the attic window, the water rising just below the windowsill, a speed boat comes along, and the pilot offers to rescue him.

"No," the man shouts over the noise of the rushing water. "The Lord will provide."

Finally, he makes it to the roof. As the water swirls around him, a helicopter hovers overhead.

"We'll throw you a rope," the soldier hanging out the open door yells down.

"No thanks, the Lord will provide," the man responds again.

Eventually, the chap is swept off the roof and drowns in the flood. He is miffed when he meets his Maker.

He asks the Lord, "Where were you? I asked for your aid. Why didn't you help me?"

[1] Hardesty, Von. *Lindbergh: Flight's Enigmatic Hero*. San Diego: Harcourt, Inc., 2002.

"I answered your prayer not once but thrice," the Lord responded. "I sent you a canoe, a boat, *and* a helicopter."

We are provided many cues along our paths. It's up to us to recognize what is an opportunity and what is a minefield. Just noticing an opportunity is half the game. Whether to act, how to act on it, and when to act on it is the second half. We don't want to be left on the roof like the faithful but doomed man in the joke as opportunities repeatedly pass before us.

HOW TO PAY FOR COLLEGE?

As I was finishing high school, I was looking for a way to pay for college. There were five younger brothers and sisters in the house. It was a typical middle class home of the 1960s. We lived well and never lacked for anything we needed, but there was no money in the budget to send me off to the college of my choice. My dad offered to pay for half of years two, three, and four of college—if my grades suited him. Year one was on me. It was my job to figure out how my freshman year was to be financed.

My father had used the GI Bill after World War II, and that seemed like a good plan for me as well. So, within a month of graduating from high school in 1971, I rode my bicycle with two friends to the nearby US military recruiting offices. I had decided I would no longer debate with my father over whether my grades were satisfactory and, thus, worthy of his contribution toward my education. I planned to pay for college myself.

Dad was sitting on the backyard swing after work when I pedaled up to tell him I had just signed on to serve the country. He put the newspaper down and asked, "Don't you know there's a war going on?" I gave him a glib answer along the lines of, "The Army will note my Jesuit education and probably find a suitable slot for me far from the jungles of Vietnam." A week or so later I was off to basic training. By the end of the summer, I was in advanced infantry training at Fort Polk, Louisiana, Home of the Combat Infantryman.

As my training was winding down in November 1971, I was issued orders to report for transit to Vietnam. Along with a handful of other soldiers, I was packing to leave Fort Polk to go home on leave before shipping out for Southeast Asia. Shortly before we were to leave the post, our group was pulled aside. We were told that our orders had been changed. We were to remain at Fort Polk and await further word on where we would be stationed next. I learned the day before Thanksgiving that I was to report to Germany and, likely, an infantry unit.

A few weeks later, I was being processed into the U.S. Army Europe at the replacement station in Ansbach, a small town in Bavaria. A young soldier reviewed my scant army dossier. He noted that I had finished high school and asked if I knew how to type. They were looking for a soldier to work at the replacement processing station. Yep, I could type. I was told the job with them in Headquarters Company was mine if I wanted it. If not, I would be sent to an infantry unit currently living in tents in the snow. I quickly signed on and became a clerk/typist, avoiding spending part of that cold, snowy winter on maneuvers with the infantry. Joining the army, my typing skills, and luck saved me from being sent to Vietnam while providing me with funding for college.

I wasn't very good at reading cues as an 18-year-old. I did, after all, join the army when there was a war going on and nearly ended up in Vietnam. Five months later, when I reached Germany, I knew well enough to put the simple skill of typing to work to land a safer posting. I'd finally read a cue!

PROFESSIONAL CUES FROM OTHER PEOPLE'S EXPERIENCES

During my first position in a law firm 10 years later, I was still not the sharpest at reading cues and adjusting accordingly. In at least one instance, the cue resided in my head for years before the light bulb went off and I finally reacted.

I was told during my interview for an associate's position that no lawyer was expected to keep up with Jim, an extremely hard-working partner in the firm. Jim worked extraordinary hours—days, evenings, and weekends. If he scheduled a trip, there was a good chance that he would cancel at the last minute. Proof that Jim was too busy could be discovered in his desk drawer. It contained a stack of unused Northwest Airlines tickets to Denver, evidence of canceled ski trips, a sport he enjoyed.

Once I had some training and responsibility for clients, like other young lawyers in the firm, I cranked out work that resulted in 60+ hours, 5-and-a-half-days a week. No one ever really kept up with Jim. That was impossible. I learned that the only route to being thoroughly prepared for a trial was to work long, hard hours, just like Jim. So, for about 25 years, that's how I worked.

However, that stack of unused airline tickets was an obvious message. Working to the exclusion of everything else life had to offer was not healthy. Nor was it enjoyable. Fun times with family and friends were being forfeited in favor of spending more time at the office. Clients were satisfied. The bills were paid. However, at some point I figured that my effectiveness was compromised when I worked extended stretches without a decent break. Jim was on my mind when I later decided to approach my day differently. I didn't want a pile of unused plane tickets in my desk drawer.

I wasn't always a slow learner when a clue dropped in my lap. Years before I was a young lawyer, watching Jim outwork us all, I was sharp enough not to scrap my plan to return to college in exchange for a pickup truck.

Exercise #1

Missed Cues:

Name three occasions when you either failed to read the cues or did not read them to your benefit:

1.

2.

3.

COLLEGE: A BIGGER RISK THAN EXPECTED

We frequently take risks in our lives and often they turn out to be valuable learning experiences. Sometimes our decisions lead to a sour experience. Have there been times in your professional life when you took a chance on a course of action and it didn't work out?

I'll bet you can recount times when you decided to take a chance that turned into a good move, maybe even a life changer—the best decision you ever made. Recognizing the cues that drop around the edges of our day can lead to one of those conversations with ourselves. Shall I take a chance—or instead sit back and stick with what is familiar?

Here's an inspiring story of a young woman leaving a lucrative position to switch gears and chase a dream. Patty and I saw Broadway star Jessica Vosk perform at The Cabaret, a club in Indianapolis. Like many Broadway personalities, Jessica is a recording artist and has her own solo show that she takes to the road when her commitments to the theater permit. Jessica was 30 years old when she landed her first gig on Broadway in *Bridges of Madison County*. She went on to roles in *Finding Neverland* and *Fiddler on the Roof*. These parts led to Jessica being cast as Elphaba, the Wicked Witch of the West in the Broadway production of *Wicked*.

In her solo show, Jessica talked about how she arrived at this point in her life and career. As a child, she wanted to be an actress. Though interested in singing and acting, Jessica studied communications and investor relations. We learned that before she graduated from college, she was hired by a New York City financial investment relations firm. Jessica was immediately successful and well-paid, advancing through the ranks of the firm. Her singing and acting career was in her rearview mirror.

Working on Wall Street was a job that beckoned day and night. There was travel, meetings, and pressure to perform at a high level. Along the way, Jessica suffered several panic attacks. One day, she dropped a sheaf of papers on the floor of her office. Among the documents scattered on the floor was a note from her grandmother: "Jessica, I wish you a lot of luck." That moment, she explained, was the catalyst for Jessica to switch gears. Her grandmother's note provided her cue.

Jessica decided that she needed to make a change. She went to her boss and told him she had to take her life in a different direction. She eventually left her job and began singing at open-mic nights in bars and clubs around Manhattan. Jessica began auditioning, and ultimately was offered a role in a show at Carnegie Hall. Her career as a singer and actress took off.

When telling her story during an interview on ABC News, Jessica observed, “If you know that you’re meant to be somewhere else, life is far too short to not take a risk or a chance,” she said. “I know it’s a long shot sometimes; I know that it can mean disappointing people, but I promise that if you don’t go after what it is that you love, you will wind up disappointing yourself more.”[2,3]

At age 30, Jessica Vosk switched careers entirely. She walked away from a secure, well-paying position. She stopped what she was doing professionally, looked at where she was in her life, and listened to the message from her grandmother. She revisited the fork in her road and took another direction.

RISK COMFORT LEVEL

There are books and management courses devoted to the topic of risk assessment. We’re not going to go in-depth here on this. Determining the hazards and potential pitfalls is part of making any decision—the bigger the decision, the farther the possible fall. There’s a risk assessment tool for just about every decision ever made: financial, career, education, and probably deciding what to wear.

Think about your comfort level when faced with big decisions. The tolerance you have for taking risks is another facet of your planning that you will want to revisit from time to time. It may change. You want to give more than just a passing thought to where you land on the scale of risk-takers as you plot your course. Be bold—not stupid.

---

[2] Robinson, Kelley, and Emily Whipp. “From Wall Street to ’Wicked,’ How This Broadway Star Risked It All To Defy Gravity.” *ABC News*. September 24, 2018. https://abcnews.go.com/Entertainment/wall-street-wicked-broadway-star-risked/story?id=57937051.

[3] Brunner, Jeryl. “From Banking To Broadway: Jessica Vosk Ditched Her Finance Career To Perform On The World’s Greatest Stages Including Carnegie Hall.” *Forbes*. November 29, 2022. https://www.forbes.com/sites/jerylbrunner/2022/11/29/from-banking-to-broadway-jessica--vosk-ditched-her-finance-career-to-perform-on-the-worlds-greatest-stages-including-carnegie-hall/.

Exercise #2

Risk Comfort Level:

What is your level of comfort when it comes to taking risks? Do you:

- Accept risk?
- Avoid risk?
- Attempt to reduce risk?
- Transfer your risk to others?

How daring will you be when it comes time to make a change in your life?

ATTENDING COLLEGE IN FITS AND STARTS

In early 1973, my commitment to the U.S. Army was winding down. I planned to return to Indianapolis and start college. Patty and I had been corresponding during my time in Germany, and we spent time together when I was home on leave.

Patty Lykins and I grew up in the same neighborhood. We attended the same school, our parents were friends, and we'd known each other since I was 12 years old. By the time I was discharged from the military, I was not quite 20 years old and we had been friends for a long time, but other than going to see a movie, *Butch Cassidy and the Sundance Kid,* and a Beach Boys concert, we'd never really dated before I left for basic training. During the period that I was in the service, we grew closer.

I wrote Patty often, once or twice a week. I looked forward to her letters that I received several times a week. Occasionally I would call home from Germany, which at the time was incredibly expensive. Because of the time difference, Patty would go to my parents' home on her way to school and join in on the call. After we were married, Dad needled me about the $50 collect calls made to my girlfriend on his phone bill.

Upon my return from Germany, I worked for a short time at my old job delivering flowers before being hired at a wholesale florist, Cleveland Plant and Flower. There I helped fill orders and eventually had a route delivering flowers to shops around central Indiana. I had to be at work at 6 a.m. but I was off around noon so I could take some college courses. When a better route with a larger truck and commission-based pay opened, I put in for it. The boss, George, gave the job to one of my coworkers. I was upset. I wanted that route, I wanted to drive the big truck, and I really wanted the cash that went along with the more lucrative position.

George was looking out for me. He knew I was going to school. Putting me on that route would have caused me to postpone my plan to go to college, maybe forever. Though hard to swallow at the time, my colleague had more experience and was, in fact, the better pick for the truck route. George did me a favor I wasn't able to appreciate at the time by leaving me in a position that would be easier to quit in favor of my education.

I started college in the fall of 1973. A career in medicine was what I had in mind. However, my inability to master the slide rule while in high school rendered me ignorant of chemistry. I guess that I believed that the nearly two years I spent in the army had somehow infused my brain with math and science skills. I discovered quickly that wasn't so. My career plans crashed when my grades included a D in a five credit hour course in zoology. My medical career was doomed at the end of my first semester of college.

The next fall I decided to study business. A week or two into my third semester of college, I discovered that the only way I could get a balance sheet to balance was by plugging in a number. The accounting instructor was not amused. I dropped out of college a few weeks into the semester.

I quickly found a job filling vending machines, and Patty started studying at Indiana Central Beauty College. For us at the time, I was making big money—$185 a week. As a candy man, I enjoyed the added perk of all the Twinkies and candy I could eat. It wasn't medicine or business, but I was working.

Exercise #3

Personal Failures:

Name three personal failures you've dealt with:

1.

2.

3.

LOOKING FOR AND FINDING INSPIRATION: WHERE DO YOU START?

We are bombarded with information from multiple fronts. Sorting through it can be overwhelming at times. We also absorb data from our daily exposure to people and events. Buried in the barrage of material we soak up every day are snippets that really grab our attention, pique our interest to learn more, and move us to act. What has inspired you to take a course of action?

Inspiration can come from anyone, anything, and anywhere. Here are some success stories that may resonate and inspire you to get moving. I took inspiration both from old guys as well as a 30-year-old woman. You may even learn a thing or two from the people living in your own home. It's never too late to get started. We just have to get off our duffs, as Dad would say.

A few years ago, I developed an attraction to the work of Marcel Pagnol, an accomplished Frenchman born in 1895 and raised in Marseille. I was familiar with his books and some of his movies. However, my interest in learning more about Marcel was piqued when I discovered how this fellow reinvented himself in his sixth decade on the planet. I was closing in on my 60s myself when I learned how Marcel began yet another career at about that same point in his life.

As a young man, Marcel was a teacher, writing plays in his spare time. He became a successful and well-known playwright in 1920s Paris. Marcel foresaw talking pictures becoming popular, so he switched gears. He became a famous director, bringing to the screen—and a much wider audience—some of the plays that had made him famous at the outset of his career.

The playwright-turned-movie-producer and studio head was 62 and retired when a friend asked him to put pen-to-paper for *Elle Magazine* some of the stories about his youth that he had told around the dinner table. The first edition with his short story flew off the shelves. Marcel's serialized story of his summers spent in the hills around Marseille gained broad interest. He acted on this success. Marcel developed the short stories into a two-volume memoir. He capped his literary career with two more books, published when he was 67 years old. The works became classics and have twice been made into movies. He even had two books published posthumously. That's what I call a successful author.

Marcel changed gears and dove into a project that had grabbed his attention when he was 62 years old. In the process, he added to his legacy in a field that was new to him at an age when some folks are napping after a round of golf.

IT'S NEVER TOO LATE

Here is one last, quick story for those who are saying to themselves, "I've waited too long. I can't switch gears at this point in my life. It is what it is." The late U.S. Supreme Court Justice John Paul Stevens was born in 1920. He was appointed to the Supreme Court by President Gerald Ford in 1975. Justice Stevens retired from the Court in 2010 when he was 90 years old. After he retired, he authored three books. His last work was published when he was 99 years old.

My mom, who lived to be nearly 91 years old, frequently said, "Age is just a number." She was right.

Your stage in life is not a roadblock to you making changes unless you allow it to be.

There's no "Old Guys Rule" T-shirt in my closet. It's a clever phrase. It sells T-shirts, other merchandise, and probably tattoos. I doubt I will ever buy one. Some of the fellas I see wearing the T-shirt look different than the trim, fit models on the website. There's a message in the slogan. What I glean from the phrase is that old guys and girls can rule—as in, rule their lives.

"Old" as pertains to a man or woman is a relative term. It is not necessarily a function of one's chronological age. It is sometimes difficult to define. We know old when we see it, but when is one truly old?

Have you allowed your age to determine what you can accomplish?

Physical limitations apply, as they always have. I could never dunk a basketball. I never even touched the rim. So, if you think you want to climb a mountain and are out of breath walking a mile, modify your goal. Better yet, train for it.

I hit a point in life when I began to marvel at what those who I once considered "old guys" had accomplished when they were the "old guys." As I'd stew about not writing that book on legal ethics I could have when I was 50, I discovered Marcel Pagnol started his writing career in his 60s. John Paul Stevens was writing books way into his 90s. Jessica Vosk described walking away from Wall Street at age 30 to chase her dream and become a singer.

How did they do it? Why are they different than me—or you or anyone else who aspires to make a change? The answer is perhaps simple. They got up one morning and got started. Sometimes we just need to take the plunge

Exercise #4

Inspiration:

Name three sources of inspiration you've encountered in your life (person, book, movie, event, incident):

1.

2.

3.

Now, when I look back, I realize I didn't actually look back. Not soon enough anyway. Sure, it worked out for me, but you can begin sooner than I did. My reflection was haphazard and unorganized. You could say it was a bit fly by night. Putting the pencil to it with my career coach Mark forced me to assess what I had to offer myself. When I now review my wish list of what I then thought I might want to do, it was less random than I had imagined.

What seemed like an exercise in which I scattershot my goals was, in fact, more deliberate. Mark asked me to dream big, to set no limits, and not to exclude anything I might want to achieve. Only a few things on my list were not attainable. Turns out my list is a reflection of my underdeveloped skills, dormant talents, and unmet goals. Subconsciously, I reflected on what I brought to my table. Thinking more strategically early on would have yielded a road with fewer ruts.

KRISTI DOSH: THE SPORTSBIZ MISS

Kristi Dosh wanted to be a lawyer since she was five years old. She finished high school a year early so she could start law school sooner. When she graduated from the University of Florida Law School in 2007, Kristi was hired by the law firm where she hoped she would land. Her legal career was off and running according to plan.

Law wasn't Kristi's only passion. Her interests included sports and writing. Along the way, Kristi nurtured her writing talent and kept her passion for sports. One day her outside-of-the-office interests would be companions to her law degree.

During law school, Kristi penned an article about the business side of the sports world. Several years later she came across a video clip on a related topic by *Forbes*, but she disagreed with the analysis. Kristi's email to the editor to share her viewpoint resulted in the editor's offer for Kristi to write for *Forbes*.

Initially, her gig with *Forbes* did not pay, but Kristi kept at it. She added other publications to her portfolio such as *The Washington Post* and *Sports Business Journal*. Kristi began to be paid for her writing. During the next few years, Kristi was asked to do podcasts and appear on a Comcast program *SportsNite*. This led to her own weekly segment *Miss SportsBiz*.

One day an agent friend of Kristi's told her she should go to New York to meet with a producer at ESPN. She flew from her home in Atlanta, believing it to be a networking opportunity. Halfway through her visit with the producer, she realized she was being interviewed. Before she left New York that day, Kristi was told they'd be making her an offer to join ESPN as a sports business reporter. The position came with more money than her current four-year associate's salary as well as a platform from which Kristi launched a successful media career. She was in high demand for radio, television, and podcast interviews to discuss the business of sports.

Kristi moved on from ESPN after her two-year contract was up. By then she was a successful blogger and author. Kristi's college football book, *Saturday Millionaires: How Winning Football Builds Winning Colleges,* was published in 2013.

Until taking on the challenge at ESPN, Kristi never thought of combining her interest in the law with writing and sports. All her passions were combined into a full-time job. Today, Kristi is an entrepreneur wearing multiple hats. She fills her days as a speaker and consultant, teaches at the University of Florida, and hosts two podcasts. Kristi is an experienced travel writer and co-founder of several travel websites. She also makes time for her romance novelist career as Savannah Carlisle.

Now 15 years out of law school, Kristi continues to reinvent herself. Her law degree was the springboard launching Kristi's sports media career. By keeping her eyes open, taking risks, and sometimes working for free, Kristi Dosh landed a career that melded the law with her passions. Her glide path took her a long way from an associate's desk and the lawyer life she aspired to as a girl.

Kristi's secret: she is continually looking *over* the horizon. She told me: "Too many lawyers put on blinders and just keep their heads down. They miss loads of opportunities."[4]

---

[4] Kristi Dosh, *the SportsBizMiss*. Accessed April 26, 2023. You can learn more about Kristi Dosh at https://www.kristidosh.com.

PART II

Chart Your Journey

As we meander down the road of our lives, opportunities present themselves. Some we seek. Others find us. Too many choices sometimes frustrate our decision-making. Making the correct choice is not an art form. It's a process by which we can learn.

> "A person who never made a mistake never tried anything new."[1]
>
> —Albert Einstein, German physicist (1879–1955)

---

1 BrainyQuote. "Albert Einstein Quotes." Accessed April 26, 2023. https://www.brainyquote.com/quotes/albert_einstein_148788.

4

Finding *My* Landing Zone

> "Success is not measured by what a man accomplishes, but by the opposition he has encountered and the courage with which he has maintained the struggle against overwhelming odds"[1]
>
> —Charles Lindbergh, American aviator (1902–1974)

I've long had an interest in Charles Lindbergh. In college, I read his book and biographies about him. A friend gave me a collection of old postcards featuring the celebrated pilot and his airplane, The Spirit of St. Louis. A complicated figure later in his life, as a young man he was thrust into the limelight after flying a small plane across the Atlantic Ocean. Overnight he became a hero.

Before his flight to Paris, Charles was experienced in flying over land. He navigated using landmarks on the ground, such as lakes and cities. Before his voyage across the Atlantic Ocean, Charles did a great deal of studying and planning. He secured material accumulated by the U.S. Hydrographic Office detailing information about currents, prevailing winds, and air pressure. With this information, he created a chart to guide him through the night across the sea to France. To verify that his calculations were accurate, Charles double-checked his map after first learning trigonometry from library books. He arrived at his landing zone in Paris, 33 and a half hours after leaving New York, guided by the route he had painstakingly plotted.

1 Hardesty, Von. *Lindbergh: Flight's Enigmatic Hero.* San Diego: Harcourt, Inc., 2002.

Charles put a lot of work into finding his landing zone. He was purposeful. His preparation was meticulous. However, he still cast-off to cross the ocean on a voyage many predicted would end in failure, as it had for many other pilots who attempted the trip before him. It took courage to do something no one had ever done before. It also took imagination, and, most importantly, it took planning.

Charles wasn't my role model when it came to devising a strategy for how to manage my future. I never had the discipline to attempt to teach myself trigonometry in the public library. The preparation in which he engaged to successfully complete his daring feat puts Charles in a different league than me when it comes to planning skills.

My route to the legal profession was along a winding road. Once in the door, it became a meandering path through the law business. Sections of the road I took have the appearance of being part of a strategic plan. Others, not so much. At the outset, I had no clear focus. There was no role model after whom to pattern my future as a lawyer. Unlike Charles, I had no navigational chart to follow toward my landing zone. Ultimately it may not have mattered, but with more introspection and better planning, it could have been a smoother ride.

GETTING INTO LAW SCHOOL

In 1977, I applied to law school. I was promptly put on the wait list. I visited the school's dean of students. When I met with him to learn why I was on the wait list—and what that meant—his advice to me was "don't panic." He asked that I come to visit him again with my grades after my last semester of college. The dean also told me to work on a plan B. That was not encouraging.

To finish college and start law school in the fall, I was enrolled in 20 credit hours of courses during my last semester. When the spring semester was over, I revisited the dean as planned. I had my transcript in hand, reflecting a 4.0 GPA for my final semester. He was complimentary but noncommittal. For a second time he told me to keep my options open. I would hear if my "wait-listed" status would change—admitted or rejected—before the fall semester began in three months.

A couple of weeks before classes started, I received a letter admitting me to law school. I was in! I still remember walking up the front steps of the law school alongside a classmate on the first day of classes. It was a sunny morning in August 1977. I was 24 years old and on top of the world, as they say. It was a great moment for me.

MORE DIFFICULTIES TO OVERCOME: THE UPS AND DOWNS OF LAW SCHOOL

Whether it's lessons from your past or potential mistakes looming in your future, we need to recognize that complete security while making our decisions isn't always possible.

Getting into law school was the first step. When my first set of grades was posted, I wondered why I had put so much effort into getting into law school. I ended the first semester with about half the GPA I had achieved in the last semester of college. There was a D in Contracts glaring at me from my transcript. I mulled over what to do next as I entertained thoughts of dropping out of law school.

Friends counseled me. "Mac, you just took yourself out of the running for a job at any of the big firms in town. You'll never recover your GPA to the point that you'll be considered. Forget about that career path. Get over it. What you need to do is pick yourself up, get better grades, and meet as many people as you can while you're in law school."

The dean thought differently about how I might change the trajectory of my GPA. He told me to quit my part-time job, cut back on my involvement in student government and work on the school newspaper to better focus on my studies. I had immense respect for the dean, who I came to know well. He offered me a fair amount of fatherly advice during my time as a law student. Nonetheless, in a brilliant example of *not* taking other people's advice, I became more involved in student government. In my third year of law school, I was elected president of the Student Bar Association. It was a great way to meet many of my fellow law students and interact more with the faculty and administration.

Frankly, there was no way that I could not work. My veterans benefits ran out after my first year of law school. Patty and I had bills to pay. It never occurred to me to take out a student loan. From an economic viewpoint, I've always been glad that I didn't. I suppose I could have followed the dean's good advice. I could have stopped working, borrowed money, and cut back on my extracurricular and social activities. I probably would have had better grades. Looking back, I'm not certain better grades alone would have made any difference in where I ended up. I found my way despite my lackluster law school performance.

Exercise #1
Major Difficulties:

Name three major difficulties that you overcame:

1.

2.

3.

HUMBLE BEGINNINGS IN THE LAW PROFESSION

I had several friends who worked as bail commissioners out of a dingy office inside the county jail. I applied and was hired for this part-time gig. The function of a bail commissioner was to interview arrestees to determine if they qualified for release without bond. There were times the bail commissioner appeared in court, addressing the judge about the merits of a release or not. I saw this as my ticket to appearing in a courtroom. The bail commissioner's court appearance was all of two minutes. The contribution to hearings was minor and mundane. However, it was a suit-and-tie job and I would speak in court. This was far more exciting than idling away in the back row of torts class.

In February of 1978, near the beginning of my second semester of law school, the Indiana Supreme Court Disciplinary Commission was looking for a law clerk who was a second- or third-year student. I applied even though I was only in my first year and had an interview with the Executive Secretary of the agency, Sheldon Breskow. Halfway through the interview, I noticed that I was wearing two different color socks. Sheldon overlooked my lackluster GPA and my fashion faux pas. I resigned from my bail commissioner's post when Sheldon told me he would give me a shot at the job. I was hired along with a second-year student and we shared the law clerk position, both working part-time.

Thankfully, the dean permitted students to take day and night classes. This helped those of us who had to work while attending law school. The boss allowed us to work around our class schedules. I kept that job throughout law school.

My time in law school flew by. I planned to take the bar exam in February 1980. Taking the bar review course was essential to improving the odds of taking the exam only one time. It cost money, which was not abundant. A popular professor ran the bar review course. I was fortunate to have been hired by the professor to help him put on the program. In exchange, he comped my tuition for the course. Along with another student, our job was to tape-record the program on massive reel-to-reel recorders. We then boxed the tapes and drove them to the bus station after each class. The recorded program was shipped to the state's other law schools to be played to other groups of future lawyers preparing for the bar.

In February 1980, I sat for the bar. The setting was the Murat Temple in Indianapolis, the ornate home of the Shriners. The room where the test was taken was massive. Despite the distractions of the Egyptian artwork across the wall and the two examinees in the row in front of me leaving for lunch and not returning, I passed the exam. In May, the Chief Justice of The Indiana Supreme Court swore me in to the bar. I was a lawyer.

THE SEARCH FOR FULL-TIME WORK

The market for new lawyers was tough in May 1980, the year I graduated from law school. I peppered about 80 central Indiana law firms with my résumé. I received in return more than 50 rejection letters. I never heard anything from the other firms and governmental agencies with whom I had sought work. This was another awakening. What the hell was happening here? Beginning with my first career at age 10, delivering the *Indianapolis Times*, I had never had a problem finding a job.

At the time I had been a law clerk for the Disciplinary Commission for two years. The boss offered me the opportunity to stay on as a staff attorney, which I accepted. I had developed a great relationship with Sheldon during my time at the commission. He had taken me under his wing. I learned a lot from him and I liked the work. Believe it or not, Sheldon and I even shared a tea bag from time to time. I guess they were in short supply.

Sheldon's job offer had one string attached. He told me that I could have the position for one year and only one year. After a year, Sheldon said, "You need to get a job with a firm. I don't want you to be a government lawyer like me." His comment struck me and has stuck with me. Here was a man appointed to his position by the Indiana Supreme Court. Sheldon previously held a senior position in the office of the Indiana Attorney General. I would have been pleased to have had his career. If Sheldon told me why he made that observation, I've long forgotten. Like other advice he gave to me, it turned out to be sound.

I signed on and Sheldon continued to be a great influence in my life. I was elevated from law clerk and became a staff attorney at the Indiana Supreme Court Disciplinary Commission. The agency investigates claims of attorney misconduct. Some of the cases go to trial before a hearing officer appointed by the state Supreme Court. I began to learn about being a trial lawyer. I traveled across the state, investigating cases.

Though not planned that way, I tried my first case with Sheldon at my side. I had been assigned a case which I worked up and prepared for trial with the help of Sheldon and the other more experienced staff attorneys. There'd been no talk of co-counsel. On the morning of the trial, I took my place at the counsel table in the Indiana Supreme Court conference room, where the hearing was to take place. Every question for every witness was written out on my legal pad. My rule book was open on the table. I was wearing my best—and only—suit. I was ready for battle.

The lawyer who was charged with misconduct faced me across the room. Next to him defending the case was a senior partner in the biggest law firm in the state. This seasoned litigator was no doubt also ready for the courtroom battle. They sat looking at me, knowing I had been admitted to the bar less than a month ago.

I was about to call my first witness when the oak door behind me creaked. It opened just enough for Sheldon to squeeze through it. He exchanged pleasantries with everyone as he took the chair next to me. Before I could ask my first question, he slid the pad with my notes on the witnesses to his side of the table. Then he whispered that he'd question the witness. There were no grand tales to brag about from my first trial. I went from lead counsel to second-chair lawyer and scrivener in seconds. That was okay. I had no business going toe-to-toe in a lawyer discipline case with the chief litigator from a big law firm. I would have plenty of days in court to look forward to ahead of me.

At the end of my one year as a staff attorney, the job market was not much better than it had been in 1980. As the spring of 1981 came along, I once again showered the Indianapolis legal community with my résumé. In a repeat of my previous year's dismal performance, I began to collect a pile of rejection letters. I needed a plan B, fearing Sheldon was serious about my one-year deal.

THE INDIANA-FRANCE CONUNDRUM

As my year as a staff attorney at the Disciplinary Commission wound down, I was 28 years old and Patty was 26. We had no children and had been free to travel when finances, work, and school allowed. Much of that travel was to our beloved France. We had developed an interest in Europe, and in particular France, which we'd visited three times. Patty and I mused about what fun it would be to live in France, though we had no clue about how that could be accomplished.

Panic began to set in as my second effort at finding an associate's position was yielding no prospects. Then I stumbled across a Master of Laws (LLM) program in international business based in Salzburg, Austria, offered by the University of the Pacific's McGeorge School of Law and saw a glimmer of hope. Students in the program studied first in Austria before working as interns in various European cities. Here, I thought, was our ticket to living in Paris. This also became my backup plan in the event

I could not find a position with a law firm and Sheldon held true to his promise to boot me after one year.

I was accepted into the program and we were excited about the prospect of a European adventure. Then things got complicated. As we were sorting out the logistics of our move to France, I received a call out of the blue from a law firm in a small Indiana town in the next county from our home. They had my résumé and wanted to talk.

I had never heard of the firm and had not sent my résumé to this respected county seat practice. Several years later, I learned how that call came about. Jim, my boss and mentor-to-be, called a lawyer friend in Indianapolis and asked whether he knew of any candidates for an associate position. This lawyer didn't know me. We'd never met. He had received my resume as part of my unsuccessful approach to finding a job by peppering the town with my résumé a year earlier. In response to Jim's inquiry, his friend pulled my résumé from his file and put it into Jim's hands. I ended up with a job offer.

Within a few weeks, I went from having no job prospects to two competing and totally different opportunities. I had a job offer to work in a small town in Indiana and a position waiting for me in Paris, France. Now what to do? I went to Sheldon and told him of the dilemma I had created for Patty and me.

When pontificating, my lanky boss stretched out in his chair. Over his shoulder, the shining, copper dome of the Indiana Statehouse gleamed out the window. Sheldon regularly trimmed his nails when we chatted. He would lean back in his chair, put his feet on his desk, and pull out his nail clippers. When he was ready to make his point, he would put the clippers down, pull his feet off the desk, lean forward, and point his long index finger at me for emphasis. That day was no different.

Sheldon dove in to help me come to a decision. "McGoff, you only get two bad moves in this career," he said as he dropped his clippers. "You've got to be picky." He told me, "You won't recover from a third bad career decision." We analyzed the facts together. The McGeorge School of Law LLM program offered a degree in international business. I was a history major that dropped out of accounting 101 when I couldn't get a balance sheet to balance. On the other hand, the position in Greenfield presented the opportunity to learn how to be a trial lawyer.

Exercise #2

Decisions, Decisions, Decisions:

1. Have there been personal or professional opportunities that came your way and put you in a quandary about which path to follow? Write down two or three of the decisions that you're happy about.

2. Next, give some thought to a few times an offer came your way that you passed upon. Are you now kicking yourself for doing so? Did you make the correct decision?

3. Are there experiences or decisions you envied others for undertaking? Write these down.

ARE THERE DECISION PATTERNS IN YOUR PAST?

So why dig back and conjure up old memories, good or bad? There are secrets to the path forward lurking in the back of our minds. Talent is hibernating, forgotten in the crush of day-to-day life, just waiting to be ignited again.

Not all that long before Sheldon steered me to making a good decision in choosing between Paris, France, or Greenfield, Indiana, I had a supervisor who tried to lure me to another career. He tempted me with the promise of a blue pickup truck. This offer was less alluring than moving to Paris, but to this day I'm reminded of the bait used to lure me.

In 1975, only six years before I became an associate in a law firm, I was at a quite different place in my life. Unable to find direction after one year of college, I decided to sit out a year and work while Patty attended beauty college full-time to become a hairdresser. I found a job filling candy machines at a local vending company.

Outside the massive warehouse just before 6 a.m., Monday through Friday, the drivers lined up. We were all dressed in dark blue slacks. On our light blue shirts, our names were emblazoned over one pocket and the company name over the other. We were required to be there before sun up. When the door popped open at 6:00 a.m. sharp, we would go straight to our trucks and hit our routes.

On my route was Indiana University Hospital, several high schools, small factories on the west side of Indianapolis, and numerous filling stations. I'd blaze in with my cart full of chips, pastries, and candy, and fill the machines as quickly as possible. Once I had completed my route, I'd return to the shop, turn in the bags of money each machine had generated, and fill up my truck with product to be ready to roll the next morning.

On most days, the early start meant an early finish. This allowed time in the afternoon to pick up a few hours of schooling by way of a correspondence course. A disciplined student could methodically work through a semester's class at their own pace. Tests were taken in the comfort of the pupil's living room, where the honor system was employed against cheating. The undisciplined student, on the other hand, would find more interesting ways to fill his free time. Sliding two cans of beer down each sleeve of an army field jacket before sneaking into Indiana Pacer basketball games and loafing with boyhood buddies on the porch were more alluring pastimes than my correspondence course. These diversions, along with life in general, interfered with my correspondence course in U.S. history. I never finished it.

My salary covered our expenses. At that time, our rent was $165 a month. The car payment was $48. With me now making $185 a week, we were living well. We liked the money. A traffic jam or a malfunctioning candy machine were about the only stress inducers I encountered in my candy man life. The somewhat carefree lifestyle was appealing and easy for me to fall into, but I knew being a candy man was not my calling.

We had friends, family, and interesting neighbors in the apartment complex where we lived that year. An infielder for the Indianapolis Indians could be found at the pool killing time before the evening's game and the call for him to report to the major leagues. A few doors down lived two law students, Bob and Ed, who seemed to spend all their time reading. They sat sunning themselves on their patio with huge books on their laps. I'd wander down and pester them occasionally.

Ed and Bob never chased me away. They put their books aside and talked to me about their studies and law school in general. They piqued my interest and sparked a thought about my career plans, of which I had none at that moment. They gave me advice about preparing for law school. I decided that I would finish college, which I had barely started, and then apply for law school. I re-enrolled at Indiana University and planned to tell Dave, who managed the drivers, that I was hanging up my candy man shirt to pursue a career in law.

I liked Dave. He was a good boss. When I told him I was quitting, he sat me down and let me know that he was disappointed in my decision to leave the vending business. He expressed that I had done well in my nearly one year on the job. He said I appeared to have the makings of a future supervisor and he requested that I reconsider. Dave also asked if I was aware of how difficult it would be for me to get into law school. He suggested, and not subtly, that I probably wouldn't make it. Then where would I be? Dave dropped his voice and enticed me with, "Kevin, you do know that supervisors are allowed to take their company pickup trucks home for personal use after hours and on weekends, right?"

I didn't take the bait. I wasn't really tempted. I have always thought that it was a nice try by Dave. He had an easy mark in me at the time. I was a 23-year-old member of a one-car family. I had no clear sense of direction. Telling me it was unlikely I'd be accepted into law school and dangling a pickup truck was a good last-ditch effort to keep me in the uniform of a candy man.

Over the years, I'd share with Patty the travails of a difficult case or maybe just whined after a bad day. She would kindly remind me that I could have had the pickup truck. Though I never did get my pickup truck, that is one road I am glad I didn't take. It is important to be alert to offers bringing short-term satisfaction that do not fit with the long-term plan.

Exercise #3

Second-Guessing Yourself:

Describe a situation when you doubted a decision you made. What did you do to deal with it? Accept or change it?

SMALL TOWN INDIANA PRACTICE

It was a 25-minute drive from our house to my new law firm's offices on the courthouse square. After I had a couple of interviews, Patty and I were shown the town on a Sunday afternoon by one of the attorneys. I was offered and accepted a position as an associate, and Patty and I took off to France for two weeks before I started my new job.

One of the partners, Jim (whom I have referred to) was a brilliant trial lawyer. After I was at the firm for a short while, he took me under his wing. Jim was well-known for his work as a criminal defense lawyer and as a divorce lawyer throughout the eastern part of Indiana. The partners had more business than they could handle. This enabled me and the other young lawyers to have more than enough work on which to begin to learn the ropes.

I enjoyed the practice of the law in this county seat office. The firm took on a variety of cases and legal problems. The partners were all successful, and there were plenty of opportunities to be a part of any type of matter one could imagine. I worked on bankruptcies and guardianships, set up a few corporations, and even wrote a few wills. Most of my time was devoted to litigation. The experience I gained and the mentoring I received from the partners and more experienced lawyers at the firm rapidly moved me forward in my career. In the early days, I was in someone's office three or four times a day, asking questions and looking for guidance. Sometimes my questions were basic, but I was never kicked out or discouraged from seeking help. Soon, I was sitting second chair in civil and criminal jury trials. After a few years, I was trying cases on my own.

I learned much from Jim. I did research, drafted legal memorandums, interviewed witnesses, and helped him prepare for trial in cases where our clients were charged with serious crimes. I was soon at the counsel table and responsible for questioning witnesses in murder prosecutions we were defending. I learned like most young trial lawyers—by going to court. At first, I cross-examined the easy witnesses, like the coroner. I sliced into their damaging testimony with cross-examination along the lines of, "Sir, you testified this was a homicide, but you did not witness this person's death, did you?" I had a lot to learn.

Eventually, I graduated to assisting Jim in jury selection and examining more challenging witnesses. As we prepared for trial, Jim and I would go over the witness list. Jim would ask, "Which ones do you want?" Though I could have my pick, I knew my limitations. I was apprehensive about being responsible for questioning the more important witnesses, particularly the detectives. I also knew better than to volunteer to question the lead investigators. Jim would never relinquish the opportunity to spar with them during his cross-examination anyway.

Murder trials were often big events in small Indiana communities. The local press would provide a daily summary of the courtroom goings-on. The hourly news broadcast on the town's radio station included a summary of the day's events as the trial went along. The gallery was often jammed with interested town folk, along with the families of our client and the victim. Tensions were sometimes high. One of the local sheriff's deputies kindly escorted us to the county line one night after a verdict that didn't go the way the victim's kin had hoped. I once acquired a series of dents on the door of my car. They were inflicted by the heel of a woman's cowboy boot, highlighting her displeasure with how she was characterized during our final argument to the jury. These were exciting times for me.

The firm's plan was for Patty and me to move from Indianapolis and become part of the community in the smaller county where I was working to benefit my law practice. The town was then, and is now, a nice place to live. However, Patty had her business in Indianapolis. She worked hard, getting to her shop at 6:00 a.m. some mornings to accommodate lawyers and businessmen who wanted their hair cut on their way to their offices downtown. Our families and social life were in Indianapolis. The drive to work for me was easy. It was only 25 minutes against the flow of traffic into the city, with a cup of tea early in the mornings. Occasionally, a beer would accompany me during the 25-minute ride back home at night. Ultimately, the partners appreciated that I could be an effective member of the firm while living in Indianapolis. They stopped asking when we were moving.

Exercise #4

Mentors and Heroes:

Create a list of people who have mentored you or to whom you look up to:

1. Mentor/Person you look up to:

2. Mentor/Person you look up to:

3. Mentor/Person you look up to:

Even with all his planning, there were potential obstacles Charles knew he might encounter. He had the luxury of the map he carefully created to guide him. However, the wind could push him off course. He would then likely perish, running out of fuel over the ocean. "I don't believe in taking foolish chances. But nothing can be accomplished by not taking a chance at all," he wrote.[2] He took off, heading toward the ocean and into the uncertainty of his North Atlantic crossing that long-ago afternoon.

---

[2] Hardesty, Von. *Lindbergh: Flight's Enigmatic Hero*. San Diego: Harcourt, Inc., 2002.

The winds shoving me around my career path blew from all directions. It's only because my old résumé resided in a lawyer's desk drawer for a year that I got a call that led to my first desk in a law firm. Other influences on where I was headed arose in the form of the cases and projects I undertook, the results I obtained, and the other lawyers and law firms with whom I associated.

5

Arriving at My Landing Zone

> "If you want to be successful, it's just this simple. Know what you are doing. Love what you are doing. And believe in what you are doing"[1]
>
> —Will Rogers, American humorist (1879–1935)

Now, decades after taking off on my career path, I gaze out the window as our plane lands at a large airport and I see another aircraft cruising alongside our flight. The plane seems to be barely moving. It is preparing to land on the runway parallel to ours. Across the sky, I can almost see the passengers in the windows of the dimly lit cabin. Though our travels began in cities far apart, here we are, landing side-by-side simultaneously at our chosen destination. Looking back, I see the sky filled with flickering lights. Rows of aircraft are lined up, each gliding toward the lights blinking on the runway. There they will finish their journeys in the same destination with perfectly choreographed landings, two abreast on parallel runways.

The two avenues of my personal and professional life ran along a similar trajectory. My education and then work as an attorney came from one direction. Emerging from an entirely different direction came the desire to move along and do something different. As I glided toward the end of my working days on my professional track, I began to cultivate other interests in the personal track of my life. For a few years, these bits of my life glided along together slowly, like our landing plane. They then began to run parallel and eventually met, arriving at the same destination.

---

[1] BrainyQuote. "Will Rogers Quotes." Accessed April 26, 2023. https://www.brainyquote.com/quotes/will_rogers_393804.

My days as a lawyer wound down and the plans that Patty and I had been developing simultaneously came into focus. As airplanes coming from different cities completing their journeys together, my personal and professional glide paths converged at the same destination. I landed.

Charting your course requires work on several fronts. Managing your relationship with your law firm and how that may end or be tweaked is only half the equation. Mapping out what you plan to do when your 60-hour weeks at the office are behind you is the other half. The goal is to bring them together.

IF NOT LAW, THEN WHAT?

"I may not have been really sure what did interest me, but I was absolutely sure about what didn't," wrote Albert Camus in *The Stranger*.[2] As I searched for my landing zone, I had a clear idea as to what I *did not* want to do. I no longer wanted to be accountable to others day in and day out. I wanted to set my schedule. I wanted the freedom to come and go without having to organize my activities around obligations others put on my calendar. I also wanted a different professional challenge.

I was keenly aware that I had better figure out what I was going to do—whiling away afternoons on the couch dueling over which daytime television programs to watch would not be my nonworking future of choice. Since I decided not to die at my desk, at around age 60 I began to invest time in exploring meaningful endeavors in which to engage.

I wasn't going to take up the clarinet again. My woodwind had long ago been sold. Before I quit, the instrument suffered through two lackluster years at my hands, squeaking away in the back row of Sister Mary Melita's St. Pius X grade school band. Pop bought the clarinet on my promise to practice every day. He thought the next Benny Goodman was in the back bedroom. During my brief music career, I played more baseball than music scales. The clarinet turned out to be a bad investment. Dad was not happy. Sister Melita, on the other hand, was probably thrilled to see me leave the band.

Volunteer opportunities abounded, but for me, many felt confining. Some required commitment to show up on a certain day and time—putting me back to having the schedule I wished to avoid. Volunteering

---

[2] Camus, Albert. *L'Étranger* [The Stranger]. Paris: Éditions Gallimard, 1942.

for pro bono legal projects didn't seem like much of a change. I may as well just stay with the firm if doing legal work was how I wanted to spend my time.

I could never draw, and no amount of art classes would fix this affliction. My carpentry skills are so poor that Jimmy Carter wouldn't want to hold nails for me to hammer on one of his Habitat for Humanity projects.

Eliminating the hobbies and ventures for which I didn't qualify or in which I had no interest was easy. Finding something interesting to use the skills that I thought I had wasn't all that difficult. After giving it some thought, I circled back to something obvious. As often happens, what we seek is right under our noses.

WHY NOT WRITE?

I had never thought of myself as a writer even though I had, for 40 years, done legal writing. I have produced hundreds of briefs and lots of legal memoranda. Along the way, I had articles on ethical issues appear in lawyer publications. I put together many seminars, which had to be accompanied by written materials. Writing is what most lawyers do—a lot of it. The written word—now mostly typed—is how we make our living. Writing was part of the job I enjoyed and felt as though I was halfway good at it.

Before I took up lawyering, I was engaged in other types of writing: in college and law school, I worked on the student newspapers. Also in college, I had an article published in *American History Illustrated* magazine. I liked writing, though I didn't always find it to be easy. I never took the time or had the discipline to make nonlegal writing a part of my day, week, or month.

I had spent a great deal of time in the library or at bookstores planning our trips. I read the travel section in several Sunday newspapers. I'd go through travel books and study maps to prepare itineraries for us.

Over the years, I helped friends and friends of friends by giving them advice when planning their trips to Paris or somewhere else in France. I started thinking, "Why not write about travel instead of legal ethics? Maybe I should become a tour guide and shepherd visitors around France."

Having no training as a travel writer or as a tour guide, I searched for courses on both careers. Tour guides in France must be licensed. That meant taking courses, testing, and government involvement. That was not appealing to me as there are too many hoops to jump through.

Writing travel stories, on the other hand, appeared doable. I found a travel writers' conference in Denver. After the three-day program, I had 29 pages of notes, some new friends, and a boatload of ideas for articles. I was learning a skill at a seminar unrelated to the legal profession. During the next few years, I went to travel shows and took several more courses to help me learn the art of travel writing. My travel stories have been published in print and online magazines. I was selected to contribute to a project Google was sponsoring as it was dipping its toe in the travel business. I entered an article in a travel writer's contest and won an award for my work. I was being paid to write. It wasn't a lot but I was enjoying it.[3]

LEADING TOURS

Showing friends and family around Provence is another avocation I acquired toward the end of my long days in the office. Lawyers are planners. Mapping out trial strategy, organizing when my witnesses were to show up for court, and thinking strategically had been my daily game. These were all skills, believe it or not, transferable to travel planning and tour guiding. It was an easy transition from envisioning what a day at trial would look like to organizing a group visit to the sites in Provence. I've ferried cousins, some of our kids, Indianapolis Bar Association buddies, and many other friends during their visits. Patty and I have led these groups on tours of the region where we live in France. As it has only been for friends and family, the French government isn't looking for me to be licensed.

We graduated from introducing friends and family to the charms of Provence from a van to managing a boat trip for hire. We were asked by a friend to organize a cruise on the Canal du Midi for a group of lawyers. Patty piloted the boat and I served as the deckhand. At the end of a week in the sun along the canal in the south of France, we drove home while most of the others headed back to their desks in the States. We had a great week on the boat and were paid for planning the trip and running the boat. We also

[3] My path to writing this book began with learning about travel writing. The weekend program I took, what is now called Travel Writers University, set me on a course of writing. I joined its writers' group where many tips are shared. I was encouraged and learned more from fellow members, in particular Noreen Kompanic. If travel writing interests you, check out https://travelwritersuniversity.com/.

slept for the better part of two days when we got home, recuperating from our voyage.

The thought of being a travel writer, *le guide touristique* (tour guide), or crewing on a canal barge for hire never crossed my mind in the early days of my legal career. I was inching along, focused on acquiring competence in the legal profession. Unwittingly, I was at the same time developing know-how that would later apply to opportunities presented to me further down the road. I was in training for these fun and interesting possibilities without realizing it. English mathematician Alfred North Whitehead observed that "it takes an extraordinary intelligence to contemplate the obvious."[4] I don't know that it had to do with intelligence. I found the way to a purposeful and satisfying life by taking the time for simple contemplation and honest self-evaluation. Then the path became obvious.

Exercise #1
Your Accomplishments

Name three accomplishments, professional or personal, that may inspire you to undertake a new challenge:

1.

2.

3.

[4] BrainyQuote. "Alfred North Whitehead Quotes," Accessed April 26, 2023. https://www.brainyquote.com/quotes/alfred_north_whitehead_383584.

YOU ONLY HAVE TO PLEASE YOURSELF

As you set your sights on meaningful ways to spend the day after you have stopped writing your hours on a timesheet, look close to home. It may not be necessary to go back to college to start anew. Are there interests that you'd like to pursue that you had to put aside in favor of family and career? Perhaps the passion you once had can be matched with some of the skills developed over your life as a lawyer. Give some thought to pairing something you think you would enjoy doing with the tools you already possess.

I don't want a job. I have had plenty of them along the way. Without a job, we get to do as much or as little as we choose when it comes to how the day

Exercise #2
Painful Growth

Identify three instances when you've had to let go of something in order to grow professionally or personally:

1.

2.

3.

plays out. I have sketches of unfinished stories in my notebooks. Ideas are percolating for travel adventures I hope to write about, though have not yet penned. I took a hiatus from travel writing in favor of this project. Patty says she may never take on a canal-barge-for-hire gig again. It's all okay. We're the only people to whom we are accountable. We've agreed to be easy on ourselves.

Not every new endeavor or challenge you take on after you leave the office will become a life-long avocation. Maybe you take up painting and quit after a year. So what? Taking a stab at poetry and deciding you don't like your own poems is okay. The only critic that matters is you. Allow yourself to try something new and abandon it if it turns out to be boring, tedious, or it has run its course. There is no senior partner there to complain that your effort was a waste of time or resources. Identify your interests and give them a go. Your only regret will be not trying something new. Don't disappoint yourself.

FROM BUMPY ROAD TO SMOOTH GLIDING

There was no compass in hand pinpointing my position at a given moment. For example, on my first Friday in the office as a brand-new associate, I was handed a stack of files. My instructions were to take them to the courthouse across the street and find the clients associated with these files. My clients would be, I was told, sitting outside the Circuit Court waiting for their lawyer to take up a family law issue with their ex-spouses' attorneys. I had never met these people. I was to introduce myself, explain that Jim was called away on some urgent matter, and let them know that I would represent them in the courtroom battle scheduled to take place as we spoke. The only navigational tools given me were a primer on child support law and a nudge out the firm's front door, pointing me to the courthouse across the street.

The route took shape as I was airborne, gliding through life. The trajectory from my point of departure to my landing was not linear. The checkpoints along the way were often undesignated until arrival. How it worked appears to have been by happenstance, not precision planning. But there was no fear of running out of fuel and having to ditch in the water. Unlike Lucky Lindy, I had the luxury of being able to regroup when necessary. I could collect myself after a fall. Steering back on course or switching destinations altogether happened all the time. To say the zig-zag journey ended where I intended to take off would be a stretch of the truth, but the last stretch of my glide path was gentle and the landing smooth.

CHOPSAVER: FROM THE KITCHEN SINK TO AMAZON.COM

Professional musicians Dan and Noelle Gosling played for the Indianapolis Symphony Orchestra (ISO)—he the trumpet and she the violin. After three years with the ISO, Dan had to audition for his chair as part of the symphony's protocol. The skill set a trumpeter brings to a performance is different than the skills one employs when auditioning. At the end of the process, Dan finished second. The seat Dan had occupied in the ISO was awarded to Tom Hooten, a renowned trumpet player.

At age 43, Dan and Noelle had a six-year-old son, a house, and all the bills that accompany life at that stage—and now Dan had no steady work. A few weeks after losing his job, in a conversation with a former student, Dan was told about an herb that would change the course of his life. He had never heard of *Arnica montana,* a natural anti-inflammatory product derived from sunflowers. Dan learned from his former student that it is an effective treatment for lip injuries.

The next day, Dan began researching the ingredients in lip balms that were then on the market. He started conducting experiments at their kitchen table. Though he had no science background to support inventing a lip balm, Noelle let him take over the kitchen. She figured her husband was a little depressed and decided to just "let him go" with his experiments.

Kitchen pots and pans were used to mix his trial formulas. Bottles and half-empty tubes littered the dining table and the countertops. He made concoctions using beeswax, aloe vera, honey, ginger, and Advil. On the seventeenth version, after two months of trial and error, Dan declared to Noelle, "I think I have a product." It was true. Dan's lip treatment, called ChopSaver, had been successfully developed.

The healing qualities of this all-natural herbal product are recognized beyond marching bands and musicians. Dermatologists tout the product to patients using medications that dry the lips. Likewise, cancer patients have found ChopSaver useful for the same purpose. Dan's products are sold in music stores, pharmacies, physicians' offices, and specialty shops throughout the U.S. It is also available on Amazon.com.

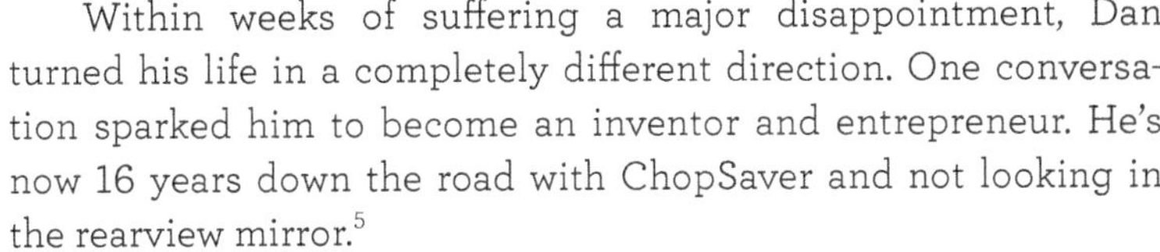

Within weeks of suffering a major disappointment, Dan turned his life in a completely different direction. One conversation sparked him to become an inventor and entrepreneur. He's now 16 years down the road with ChopSaver and not looking in the rearview mirror.[5]

---

[5] Gosling's Original ChopSaver Lip Care. Accessed April 26, 2023. https://www.chopsaver.com/.

6

Finding *Your* Landing Zone

Most every day, lawyers help clients make difficult decisions. When a client and I reached the point where it was time to report to the other side of the aisle what we wanted or whether a plea agreement or settlement was acceptable, some looked to me to make the call. I was often asked, "What would you do, Mr. McGoff?" The response I developed over time was: "There's a right decision, the wrong decision, and there's your decision." I could only be the guide; my client needed to tell me what he or she wanted to do.

> "I have been impressed with the urgency of doing. Knowing is not enough; we must apply. Being willing is not enough; we must do."[1]
>
> —Leonardo da Vinci, artist, engineer, scientist, and architect (1452–1519)

The same logic applies when it comes time to making a big decision in your life. After the research, soul-searching, and analysis is finished, you've got to make the call. Nobody is going to do it for you. It will be your decision.

THE BEST RAISE I NEVER GOT

After four years with the firm, I decided to leave to strike it out on my own. It had been a good experience for me. I liked the work and the people. But after four years, I received what I believed to be a paltry raise. I felt under-appreciated and became dissatisfied. I was working five and a half days a

[1] BrainyQuote, "Leonardo da Vinci Quotes." Accessed April 26, 2023. https://www.brainyquote.com/quotes/leonardo_da_vinci_120052.

week and had begun to develop my practice. I was no longer totally dependent on the partners to give me work. I was keeping score and knew that I was generating revenue for the partners. I had a few clients that would come with me, and I could stay in the rotation for appointments by the local judges in criminal cases where indigent defendants were provided an attorney paid for by the county.

Exercise #1

Silver Linings:

List opportunities that didn't go your way but resulted in something better:

1. Apparent failure & result:

2. Apparent failure & result:

3. Apparent failure & result:

Our personal financial footing was stable but not great. Patty's business was doing well, and our expenses were not high. We also had a family to consider. Our son was a year old, and Patty was pregnant with our daughter, Maureen. As many of you know, there is never a perfect time to make a leap as great as leaving a secure job with a paycheck to start your own business or law firm.

Wrestling with trading the certainty of a steady paycheck with the uncertainty as to when my next paying client would come along consumed six months of our lives. I likely would have stayed had the partners bumped my salary another $2,000, but my request that the number be adjusted upward slightly was not taken. I was motivated to act to change my lot. It turned out to be the best raise I never received. Moving on was good for me. It not only opened my eyes to the business of being a lawyer as a solo practitioner, but I was also steered in another direction I would never have discovered.

SOLO PRACTICE

In February 1986, I left my first law firm job along with another lawyer. He joined the practice of two friends, and I went along. The firm rented me a small office in their suite in downtown Indianapolis. The deal included the use of services such as legal secretaries. My friend and I hung our shingles, and off we went on our new ventures.

I was excited about my new arrangement. I went to the bank and opened a business account and a trust account. I found a parking space in downtown Indianapolis and ordered business cards. Patty's brother Jim sold business furniture and he helped me get what I needed to appoint a small but respectable lawyer's office. I had some interesting work and was getting paid. Once committed and on my own, the anxiety of leaving a steady paycheck slowly left the back of my mind. I fretted about the same things many solo practitioners do. Like all other solo practitioners, I learned that this was how we functioned day-to-day.

I had much to learn about office management. A few floors down from my office in the Barrister Building were a married couple that had set up a law practice together. I knew Mike from high school and had met his wife, Robyn, in law school. I spent more than a little time in their office seeking their advice about setting up a law office or brainstorming on a case where I was stuck. Mike and Robyn never turned me down and were very giving of their time. They helped me a lot.

However, in short order, I became unsettled in my new arrangement. I had work and was keeping my head above water, but I learned that, though a sole practitioner in command of my legal work, I was just a renter. I had no control over staff and no voice in office administration. I was still subject to the whims of management.

I had been accustomed to working with top-notch legal secretaries in the small-town firm where I started. I could be out of the office, confident the work I left behind when in trial or on vacation would get done. In my new arrangement, before leaving on a short trip, I left instructions for the secretary I shared with others, and for whose services I paid the firm, to prepare and file a motion for continuance in a case. When I returned, I discovered she did not file my motion. In fact she had not done any of the work I left for her. I learned that the lawyer managing the office told her to work on other matters and leave mine for later, even though one project was time-sensitive. This could have caused me a serious problem with the judge, but, fortunately, I was able to sort it out. Strike one!

The absurdity of strike two then and now still makes me chuckle. It exposed a management style with which I saw no reason to be associated. I was getting better at reading cues.

Beyond the monthly rent, I was responsible for paying the cost of long-distance phone calls. Each month, the managing partner sent the phone bill around, asking me to identify any calls I had made so that he could add the cost to my rent.

One month, the firm's phone bill listed a charge for a call made to Florida. The cost was a drop in the bucket, three or four dollars, as I recall. I had not made the call, and no one else in the office claimed to have done so either. This developed into a problem the managing partner felt compelled to delve into deeply. Who had made that call? He inquired of me more than once, and I told him repeatedly it was not my call. After much of his time and energy were spent pestering other lawyers and staff, no one admitted to having made that call. To solve the dilemma, the managing partner dialed the long-distance number to see if he could figure out who had made the call by talking to someone on the other end of the line. The managing partner ran up the firm's phone bill and riled up the entire office, spending money and wasting time trying to recover a few bucks. Strike two!

I decided that I would not wait around for Strike three. After only a few months, I could see this management style was going to be a distraction. It could also cause problems with clients and judges if this guy was going to interfere with the secretary he had assigned to me getting my work done. Now what was I going to do?

TIME TO MAKE A MOVE

About the same time that the managing partner was attempting to resolve the great phone bill mystery, I attended a criminal defense seminar. I was struggling with an issue in a death penalty case I was litigating. I knew, by reputation only, criminal defense lawyer Dick Kiefer. He was established as one of the top defense lawyers in town. He happened to be sitting a few rows ahead of me at the program.

I asked my friend Monica Foster if she knew Dick and, if so, would she introduce me to him at a break in the program. After Monica made our introduction, I told Dick I had some questions and needed help brainstorming some issues that my death penalty case presented. He offered to help and invited me to his office the next week to talk.

Dick and another attorney were sharing space in a very nice suite of offices located in an upscale suburban shopping and office complex. Dick's office was 15-feet-by-20-feet with a couch and chairs, as well as a massive desk. The walls were covered in diplomas, certificates, and photos from exotic vacations—way fancier than the narrow, bowling alley-like office I was working from in downtown Indianapolis. There was a good-sized library that was well-stocked for the needs of a litigator and criminal defense lawyer. It looked lavish, comfortable, and suggested success. I was impressed.

I figured I would get an hour of Dick's time before he'd send me on my way and get back to earning a living. He ended up spending the entire morning answering my questions and giving me help. We chatted about our families and outside interests. I left his office with some direction and ideas for handling my case. As Dick escorted me out of the door to his office, he pointed out the adjacent, empty office. He told me a lawyer had just left the group and they were looking for someone to take over the space. He asked, I thought jokingly, if I might be interested. Boy was this great timing.

Though I was looking for a new nest given my disappointment with my office-sharing situation, my first reaction was to tell Dick there was no way I could afford anything like this operation. These were established lawyers who were years into their careers with the resources to support a nice office and two support staffers. I thanked him for the offer but told him I could not afford whatever the rent might be. Dick said not to be so hasty. He told me not to focus on the cost of doing business from this suite of offices at the moment. He suggested that we meet again to explore the possibility of me taking the mammoth vacant office. We agreed that Dick would take some time to inquire around the legal community about me, and I likewise about him and his office sharing mate.

An important deadline loomed, one that today seems amusing. At the time, it forced us to do our vetting quickly. It was mid-June. How one would appear for the next 12 months in the yellow pages of the local phone book had to be determined by June 30. If you wished to change phone numbers or place an ad but missed the deadline, you were sunk. The entirety of the next year would pass without having a functional phone number listed in one of the then-primary marketing tools available. This made it difficult for prospective clients to find you. Though this seems primitive now, clients found lawyers via the phone book at that time. Appearing in the phone directory with the wrong number and wrong address could be fatal to a sole practitioner's business.

Within a week, Dick and I met to discuss terms if I were to join their office. I would be a sole practitioner, sharing space. My name would go on the door and the letterhead. I would be responsible for one-third of the common expenses. There was no way I could afford it, as I had told them at the outset. They told me that they both had more work than they could keep up with and would send business and paying projects my way. They proposed that I pay whatever I felt I could afford and build my practice. When it was sustainable, I was to tell them and then become responsible for my third of the expenses. We shook hands and it was a done deal. I happily moved to a swank suburban office and began doing business with my name on the letterhead next to the two lawyers that gave me the opportunity.

Once more my disappointment with firm management led me to explore another opportunity and led me to a move that changed my life. My good fortune in reading a cue that I was not compatible with a certain management style saved me from a career that may have been spent squabbling over office expenses.

Exercise #2

Help Finding Help

Who can help you plan the next phase of your life? If no names come to mind, write in the names of people you might ask to recommend someone who can help you.

1. Resource 1:

2. Resource 2:

3. Resource 3:

STARTING OUR LAW FIRM

My deal with my new office-sharing mates was sealed by a handshake. In the years we practiced law together, we never memorialized our arrangement in writing.

I moved my tiny desk to their well-appointed offices in the summer of 1986. That oak table desk seemed even smaller as the only bit of furniture in the huge office I was given. I was a fledgling attorney, 32 years old and not quite 6 years out of law school. I had some family law matters to work on and was defending criminal cases. I needed the phone to ring to make this arrangement work.

As promised, my new office mates gave me paying projects. I was assigned projects on some insurance defense files. Dick had been in practice for about 12 years at that point, and his criminal defense business was established and growing. He passed along clients that he didn't have the time to serve properly.

The two green ledger books from my first years of practice are still in my office at home. Thumbing through them evokes memories of my early days as a lawyer. I find that I recall something about many of the names on the pages. They also reveal that in the first year on my own, I made a little more money than I was offered to stay with my first law firm. The year-end summaries reflect how my practice grew. It was slow at first. The income inched up a bit over the next four years, as did the expenses.

After several years, I approached something of an equal to my office suite companions. Even then, my practice was more like the little brother in the business. The two lawyers with whom I shared space at the time were well-known in the circles in which they practiced and were well-established. Most obviously, they'd been at it longer. The only way for me to catch up was to keep on trying to deliver the best legal services I then knew how. There was—and is—no substitute for simply working at it. Slowly, I gained experience. I began to take on more challenging cases. My practice grew. So did our family. By the end of 1986, we had two children, and Patty cut back a bit on her hours at the shop. Two years later, we had three children.

I breathed a little easier, feeling like I had made a good decision. It was many years before I was completely comfortable that I had not just taken in my last client and that the place was in danger of folding.

During the next six years, Dick and I began to work on cases together more and more. We co-counseled criminal cases, including a death penalty case, and grew our practices separately but together. Law clerks were hired, we each brought a paralegal into our practice, and eventually, another lawyer came on board. We came to appreciate that Dick and I were like-minded in many respects, and we became great friends. We grew up in similar environments, paid our way through school, and shared the same values.

We prided ourselves in working hard—and long—hours in trying to deliver the best service to clients. Saturday mornings we were regularly in the office. It was not unusual for Dick's mom to call. If I'd answer the phone, Doris would always tell me, "You boys are working too hard. You need to go home." We didn't want to turn down business, but there were not enough hours in the day to serve our clients at the level we desired.

Financially, we were both conservative in spending our resources. I recall one lengthy discussion about whether to invest in a newfangled technology called a fax machine. Our practices, though not the same, complimented each other.

As our practices grew over the six years, we'd come to know each other's working styles and values. Eventually, both of us determined that we had outgrown the office-sharing arrangement we initially constructed and as we became displeased with the management of our operation. Dick and I contemplated making a change.

We agreed to exchange financial information. Dick and I were good record-keepers, so it was easy to compare the financial aspects of our practices. It surprised us to find that our annual revenues were nearly identical. Our interests were piqued. But before jumping into business together, we continued to share details of our income and expenses.

We determined that forming a partnership made sense for both of us to grow our practices. In 1992, we started our law firm, Kiefer and McGoff.

The formality of a partnership agreement somehow never crossed our minds. I was a history major and Dick studied political science. Law schools at the time offered no courses on law firm management. There weren't more than one or two business classes between the two of us. Our partnership was a handshake deal and remained so for the 13-plus years our firm was in operation. Dick and I never once had an argument about money.

Though we had a line of credit from which we could draw, we agreed to take no money out of the firm until we had saved enough to cover our expenses for three months. Things were a bit tight for six months, but it was a good decision. As our firm grew, our reserve increased. We used our line of credit only once in the 13-plus years we operated as K&M. If we didn't have it, we didn't spend it—or take it as a draw.

The firm grew to 10 lawyers. We usually had 3 or 4 law clerks and at least 1 paralegal. I once counted 23 employees for whom Dick and I were responsible as we were the only rainmakers. We had the good fortune to hire good people who developed into talented lawyers.

Five of our former associates are currently or have been judges or magistrates. One law clerk left the firm to clerk for the Indiana Supreme Court. He is now the senior corporate counsel at Indianapolis Motor Speedway. Four Kiefer and McGoff alumni served a term as president of the Indianapolis Bar Association, a position which I held in 2007. Lawyers from our firm have started their own law firms, hung their shingles, and served as public defenders. One is now a full-time mediator. The success Dick and I enjoyed as lawyers is in no small part due to the hard work of the lawyers we brought on board. They contributed significantly to our accomplishments and the success of the firm.

GROWING PAINS

Dick and I had great fun practicing law together and growing our firm. We had interesting work and generally got paid for it. We saw the investment of our time and resources grow over the years. As our caseload grew, we needed more assistance. As we matured in our practices, the assistance we needed called for us to seek out experienced lawyers to add to our firm. This required us to increase our payroll and develop a plan for admitting new partners if we were going to recruit and retain good lawyers. We were in the course of wrestling with these issues when two of our senior lawyers announced they were leaving to form their own firm. Dick and I were happy for them. We hated to see people leave, but we never discouraged any lawyer from departing because they wanted a different experience or desired to hang a shingle and open their own practice; that's how we started out. We found ourselves meeting on a Sunday afternoon after having just lost two attorneys, 25 percent of our office's lawyer power, contemplating the next steps. We were pushed to begin searching in earnest for our next move.

We put the pencil to it and determined that we had three choices:

1. We could shrink the firm and become more selective about what work we took in;
2. We could identify another like-sized law firm with which to merge so as to be able to afford more sophisticated management resources and to spread the cost of higher compensated lawyers among more partners;
3. We could integrate K&M into a larger firm and relieve ourselves of the management responsibilities that had us working six or seven days a week to keep up.

I suppose a fourth choice was to do nothing and keep running things as we were, but that was never seriously considered. We knew we needed to change our business model.

We hired an accounting firm to analyze our practice so that we could compare our books with other firms that may be merger candidates. We spent a lot of time brainstorming and writing down scenarios trying to come up with a solution. At first, neither Dick nor I were excited about losing control or walking away from what we had painstakingly put together for 13 years. We knew, though, we had to make some changes as there were not enough hours in the day to manage a law firm, practice law, and have much of a life outside of the office.

Exercise #3

Painful Growth:

Identify three instances when you've had to let go of something to grow professionally or personally:

1.

2.

3.

As da Vinci suggested, "we must do." Sitting around waiting for someone to make your decision won't likely happen. At times it can be a real leap of faith. Lawyers spend their days helping clients make difficult decisions. To get to your landing zone, you must pull the ripcord and take the jump into the unknown. I still buy into my own advice: "There's a right decision, the wrong decision, and there's your decision." When you are done investigating, doing the research, soul-searching, and reading the cues before you, make the call. It will be your decision and it will be the right one.

JOHN SWEENEY: BLACK BELT AT AGE 60

Over dinner one evening, John Sweeney complimented his longtime friend on looking fit and having lost weight since they'd last been out. John learned that his buddy attributed his newfound fitness to having taken up karate a few months earlier. At the time, John was feeling out of shape and carrying a few more pounds than he liked. He knew he needed an exercise outlet. His interest was piqued, and he decided to give karate a try. He was 57 years old. John trained for a couple of hours, three times a week, and it still took him a few months to get into shape. It was not easy, but he was motivated to make a change and stuck with it. Three years later, at age 60, John earned his first black belt.

His newfound fitness enthused John. He began cycling and walking more. He lost weight and found himself in better shape than he had been in years. As John's karate skills improved, he began to compete and judge at regional tournaments. He shared his passion for the sport with young beginners, teaching classes at a local Boys and Girls Club.

John's involvement in karate has brought him great satisfaction in what he has accomplished and what he has brought to his students. He is most proud of two of his young students who are nearing black belt status. John is still progressing. He achieved his 5th-degree black belt promotion at the age of 68.

This 5-degree black belt karate expert proves you don't have to be a 20-something to pick up a new sport. New interests may be presented to you at any age. If an idea comes along that sounds the least bit interesting, get your butt off the couch and give it a try. It may not be a life changing event, but then again, it might just be.

PART III

Put the Pencil to It

This section deals with the work that goes into planning your retirement or the next phase in your career. We'll also discuss implementing your plan. It includes working with your firm to create an exit plan, getting on top of your current finances, finding the right resources to plan your finances, and creating a plan that includes all of these elements so you can retire, cut back, or create a new you outside of law with minimal worry.

"A dream does not become reality through magic; it takes sweat, determination, and hard work."[1]

—Colin Powell, American statesman (1937–2021)

[1] Gracious Quotes, "43 General Colin Powell Quotes (LEADERSHIP)." Updated September 14, 2022. https://graciousquotes.com/colin-powell/.

7

Selling *My* Talents to the Firm

BIG FIRM PRACTICE

> "I think, with a negotiation, you have to go in knowing what you want, knowing what your bottom line is, and knowing what you might accept if you're absolutely pushed."[1]
>
> —Jacob Rees-Mogg, British politician

In the process of Dick and I deciding what to do next with our law firm, I contacted a friend I'd made through my involvement with the Indiana Bar Association. He was a partner at what in 2005 was among the biggest firms in the city. It also was a firm with which we were familiar. Six of my law school classmates were partners at the time. I had applied for an associate's position with the firm in 1980 and, once upon a time, had a rejection letter to prove it. My younger brother Jim, on the other hand, had lawyered at the firm before moving over to work for the state.

The firm had no criminal defense lawyers. Over the years, Dick and I received many referrals from their lawyers to handle the criminal cases they didn't take on. We were familiar with the firm and had worked with many of its attorneys. Late in the summer of 2005, we met with a team of their managing lawyers to discuss bringing our practice into their fold.

In the fall of 2005, we joined the firm as capital partners. Unfortunately, along the way, I had tossed the rejection letter from my earlier effort to join the firm. It would have been a nice conversation piece. You could say I came in through the back door. Most of our lawyers and some of our staff came with us. After signing the agreement—no handshake

[1] Quote.org. "Negotiation, Negotiations, Negotiators Quotes." Accessed April 26, 2023. https://quote.org/concept/negotiation-negotiations-negotiators-1301.

deal this time—Dick spent the weekend drafting a memo about how to manage our transition and the move to our new downtown offices on a Monday morning.

When Dick arrived at the office, a team of the firm's support staff led by the chief operating officer (COO) had already been there for hours. We met to determine who was going to do what to make for a smooth transition. As Dick began to walk through his checklist, the COO's team said to every point, "We'll do that." Finally, the COO stopped Dick and proposed shortening the meeting. He told us, "You guys go practice law. We'll take care of the rest." I had been responsible for some part of everything in my practice for nearly 20 years, as had Dick for more than 25 years. We quickly liked our decision to offload everything on our new firm's support staff, from computer maintenance, bookkeeping, hiring, and managing staff, to emptying the dishwasher.

How we worked with clients and tried cases didn't change after we joined our new law firm. There were new rules about billing, timekeeping, and such, but I quickly adjusted. Instead of working with 10 lawyers, I was now one of approximately 100 attorneys. The dramatic change was the ability to focus on my practice without the interruption of the tasks associated with being an office manager. The resources of support staff and access to talented lawyers with different fields of expertise was what we needed. Dick and I discovered that this change allowed us to elevate our practices and provide better service to our clients. Our personal lives were also enriched by culling out most of the day-to-day management obligations from our schedules.

Like any other change, you don't always get what you want. There were times when Dick and I commiserated, debating if losing control of our firm was a mistake. We both accepted that, on balance, it was a good move for both of us. We were both glad that we took the leap into a big law firm.

During the course of the next four years, I was content to practice law and speak on the topic of legal ethics at many programs throughout the state. Along with a senior staff attorney at the Indiana Supreme Court Disciplinary Commission, we developed a program to train lawyers about legal ethics. This was in the early days of the Indiana Supreme Court mandate that lawyers keep abreast of the law through continuing legal education. It became a great marketing vehicle for me. We spoke throughout the state to hundreds of Indiana lawyers every year. I grew my practice of defending lawyers and judges in professional licensure cases and advising lawyers prospectively on ethics issues. The expertise I was acquiring would serve me well in my future role at the firm.

At home, our children were finishing high school and going off to college. We spent many hours on the sidelines at soccer and volleyball matches and gymnastic tournaments. I continued my French classes for our annual trips to France. Patty and I traveled some, and she retired from her work as a hairdresser after 30 years.

THE BEST ELECTION I EVER LOST

Four years into my big law firm experience, the managing partner encouraged me to run for election to the management committee. Despite my escape from managing a law firm after we merged, I was interested in being involved in the firm's administration. In late 2009, the partners elected me to serve a two-year term on the management committee.

This turned out to be another great career experience. My bank of knowledge received another deposit that would pay a dividend down the road. The management committee approved the budget, promoted the admission of new partners, and annually met with every partner to discuss compensation and performance. The firm was courting merger candidates. I spent time on the road with other members of the firm's management, meeting with the leadership of other firms in the Midwest to evaluate the pros and cons of joining forces with other law firms. It was a lot of work on top of my practice, but I learned much in the process.

In November 2011, I was up for re-election to the management committee. A group of younger partners proposed a candidate from their ranks. When the votes were tallied, the Young Turks prevailed. Their candidate mustered more votes and replaced me on the committee. I was disappointed. It was the first election I ever lost. I stewed briefly about my electoral thumping. I appreciated the "you did a great job, tough luck" pats on the back from my partners as the post-partners' meeting cocktail party wound down. The dust quickly settled as I recognized it was time for me to move on. My failed candidacy might be a good thing.

January was always a brutal month for those serving on the management committee. There were meetings upon meetings. Compensation and bonuses had to be determined, the next year's budget set, and there were decisions to be made about the admission of new partners. Large blocks of time were scheduled for nearly every day or evening of the month. There was barely time to squeeze in legal work. There was no time for a weekend getaway to the slopes or the beach. January, as a member of the management committee, meant spending my days in a conference room, poring over documents, and adding my two cents' worth on decisions about people's careers while looking out at the gray, Indiana winter sky.

Patty and I had never been to the south of France in the winter. Now that I was going to have considerable open time on my January calendar, we were free to do so. Within a few weeks of my defeat, Patty and I booked a vacation. Though we didn't know it as we boarded the plane for Marseilles, this trip would set us on a course to fulfill a dream. I have thanked my opponent several times for knocking me off the management committee. He did me a great favor. It was the best election I ever lost.

TRANSITIONING TO GENERAL COUNSEL

In 2012, the Indiana legislature passed a law prohibiting state employees from doing business with entities owned by a close relative. My brother Jim called to ask if I was aware of the implications this change in the law would have on my law firm.

Jim is an accomplished lawyer. His expertise and advice are sought by the governor's office and elected officials throughout Indiana. After law school, he applied for and—unlike his older brother—was offered a position at the law firm that I snuck into via a merger. He was a partner when he decided upon another career path and took a job with the State of Indiana.

In 2012, when the anti-nepotism law passed, Jim was general counsel (GC) for a state agency. The agency frequently required the services of outside counsel. Jim regularly hired several partners at my firm for their expertise in managing this legal work. My brother and his team were good clients of the firm, an entity in which I had an ownership interest as a partner. The legislature's effort was meant to prevent allegations of favoritism in awarding contracts due to nepotism. The result was that Jim was no longer able to hire the firm. His brother—me—was an owner. When Jim called to break the news about the new law, he already had a plan to transition the firm's existing work for his agency to another law firm in compliance with the new law. A couple of my partners were quickly going to lose an important client.

Coincidentally, at the same time as this legislation was about to disrupt the law practices of my two partners, the managing partner and I were discussing my taking on the role of GC to the firm. We had just merged with a firm in Kentucky. Our lawyer population had grown to around 200. With five offices in three states, there was a need to have someone responsible for risk management across the firm. Also, the managing partner's responsibilities had expanded to the point where he needed to delegate certain projects so that he could better focus on running the law firm.

I had been a sole practitioner, had years of experience managing Kiefer and McGoff with Dick, and served on the firm's management committee helping steer the larger operation. My practice had had a legal ethics component to it for many years. I was a good fit to serve as GC. The timing for this discussion could not have been better for me.

NEGOTIATING MY EXIT STRATEGY

I was a 59-year-old partner in a respected law firm. I had a good practice that I had been systematically paring down for a few years. I conceded—to myself—that getting out of the criminal defense business was a good idea. After a few rough and tumble divorce cases, I began to refer all family law matters that came my way to other lawyers in the firm. I had reached a point where I could generally take on only the work that I most enjoyed.

I sincerely liked my work and the lawyers and staff I was working with, but I was still playing lawyer all the time. I was not working my way down the list of things I wanted to do that I had put together for my career coach five years earlier. Now that things had come together, I recognized this as my chance to make a dramatic change in how I was working and conducting my life. A glide path to my landing zone began to develop. This was my opportunity to construct a personalized program—to take aim at my landing zone beyond the bar.

I gave a lot of thought to my next move. I started by re-identifying the personal goals I wished to attain. We set out to thoroughly understand our family finances, and I began to entertain ideas as to what I would do with my time when 60 hours per week were opened. Patty and I spent more than a few dinners talking about the subject. I bent the ears of a few friends. Our accountant and financial advisor also weighed in for us.

I began to outline a proposal for my exit strategy. I wanted a five-year plan. This would get me to age 65. I determined what was now going to be important to me. It was a short list: I wanted clarity on the firm's financial commitment to me, more free time, and diminishing billable hours requirement.

The idea of methodically slowing down was the primary goal I wished to achieve through a new arrangement with the law firm. For the first three years, I planned to keep at it. I was not prepared financially to stop working. There was plenty of client work on my plate then and adding the GC responsibilities would have me occupied during the first part of this transition. I wanted to ease out. After 5 years of my new arrangement, I'd be 65 years young.

I drafted a memo setting forth how I wanted to spend the next five years of my life as a practicing lawyer and presented it to the managing partner. I proposed a definitive plan to take me from year three of our agreement to the exit at the end of 2018. I believed that my plan benefited the firm and suited my desires. In my pitch, I offered to relinquish my partnership interest. This would solve the firm's immediate concern of losing my brother and his agency as a client. Over time, it would free up resources by which, presumably, younger partners would benefit as another senior lawyer left the ranks of the partners.

As an employee, the firm would pick up some of the expenses I paid as a partner, most significantly a portion of our health insurance premiums. I proposed that my hours' commitment to the firm be reduced each year and that my compensation be reduced accordingly.

I produced a proposed pay scale reflecting how I believed that a reduction in my salary could be made compatible with a reduction in the hours I would devote to the firm as the GC.

This allowed me to ease my way out. During my transition, I would have more time to travel and explore other opportunities. At the same time, I could serve as the firm's GC and assist in transitioning the role to whomever the firm chose to take my place. I didn't want a hard stop to my working life. I was accustomed to working all the time. Cutting back from 60-plus hour weeks gradually made sense to me. No point in bringing a sudden shock to the system, I thought.

My compensation for the first three years was stated in our agreement. After that, my salary and hours commitment to the firm would be negotiated annually. At the end of five years, we could revisit our arrangement to determine what the firm and I wanted to do going forward.

During my time on the management committee, and after, I had many discussions with the managing partner and other firm leaders about partners' succession planning. I knew this to be an important issue for the firm. It was also my good fortune that the managing partner, governing board, and other firm leaders were progressive in their thinking about partner transition plans. We had like-minded ideas about how more senior partners could transition their practices to younger lawyers, reducing their billable hours commitment and accepting an accompanying reduction in compensation. I was not pitching a plan that I thought had no chance of success. I believed the decision makers would be open-minded about fashioning a different arrangement with the firm for me. I was correct.

We negotiated a bit, but ultimately the firm accepted my proposal. We struck a deal, memorialized it in a memo, and I went to work. I became the firm's GC with a route that began to free me up to take on new challenges outside of the law office, cut back my commitment to the firm, and engage in some leisure pursuits.

I forfeited a lot of leverage when I ceased to be a partner. It was no small thing, as I came to appreciate. I was no longer an owner with certain protections the partnership agreement afforded. However, I was secure for three years and believed I could walk away if I chose to do so in year four.

Exercise #1
What's of Most Importance to You

In order of priority, list three things you want to get out of your negotiations with your firm:

1.

2.

3.

I enjoyed my time in the role of GC. It was a position for which I was well-suited. I had been practicing in the field of legal ethics for most of my career. Over the years, I had counseled lawyers and law firms about firm structure and management. My practice was focused on litigation for more than 30 years at that point. I had encountered plenty of problem-solving opportunities along the way. With Dick Kiefer, I had put together and helped manage a small firm. After we merged, I served on the management committee and assisted in other firm initiatives. I also managed to get along with my law partners. It was the ideal time in my career to take on the work of the GC.

Counting all the lawyers in our firm, I had around 180 clients—give or take. I traveled to our various offices around the Midwest from time to time and came to know lawyers in the operation who I would never have met. Some were more demanding than others, polite but passionate. I was engaged in a variety of interesting law firm issues. There were many challenging projects that crossed my desk. I worked closely with our COO, the managing partner, and other firm leaders, helping to resolve sensitive matters. I was given a lot of responsibility and was called upon to provide input on important management decisions made during that time. I was tasked with resolving delicate issues and delivering difficult messages. That was all part of the deal. It was a good gig, and I enjoyed it. I am grateful that I had the opportunity. It was the best law job I ever had.

CRUISING CLOSER TO THE DOOR

As I said, my salary had been established for each of the first three years of my arrangement. By agreement it dropped a bit each year. In 2016, it was time for me to plan the next three years. I envisioned 2018, when I would be 65, as probably being my last year in the game. I pitched a program to the managing partner to cover what I thought would be my three remaining years with the firm. I proposed that each year I would reduce my time a bit more. Correspondingly I proposed that my compensation reflect my diminishing time in the office doing the firm's work. During year three, I would help the firm identify my replacement and assist with the transition to a new GC. We agreed that my commitment to the firm as GC would be 600 hours during my final year, 2018. I still had client work and new clients were asking for my services. If I wished to continue to do client work, that was up to me.

Once my arrangement was confirmed, I promoted what the firm and I were doing as an experiment to other senior lawyers in the firm. At about the same time, our firm was implementing compensation plans designed to encourage senior lawyers to transition their practice to the next generation. The program I developed with the firm for myself seemed like a fair way for me to move gracefully out the door. I encouraged others to consider the benefits of talking to the managing partner and jumping onto one of the firm's senior lawyer transition plans.

I continued the transition of my practice to younger partners. I was compensated for working on client matters and for bringing in business by receiving a percentage of the receipts. I knew this would diminish as I began to work less and delegate work or simply refer the business to other lawyers. This worked well for me, the law firm, and the young partners who appreciated having the work and billing credits in their columns. It helped them look good at compensation time.

Patty and I were able to spend more than two or three weeks at a time traveling. We spent a month in Mexico. We had several month-long stays at the apartment in Provence we had purchased. As the firm's phone system operated through the Internet, my desk phone rang on my computer. With six offices in three states, it was rarely important that I be physically present to answer a question. People knew that I could always be reached. It didn't matter in which office I was taking a call or in what part of the world for that matter. I was always responsive when a call or email lit up my screen. When overseas, the time difference resulted in me sometimes being on the phone at 10 o'clock at night. That was the trade-off, which was well worth it.

My work was being done. There were no complaints about my periodic absence from the country. The wind-down was working for me, although there were a few bumps on the road that I should have foreseen. Even late in the game, there is room for another missed clue.

The impact of outside influences on how I landed was unforeseen. It never crossed my mind that relinquishing my partnership would operate substantially to my benefit. When we merged Kiefer and McGoff, my plans did not envision becoming the firm's GC. It never occurred to me that the Indiana legislature would directly influence my career decisions. No amount of planning could have prepared me for finding opportunities in the events that collided at the very moment I was seeking to find a path for gliding out of the practice of law and moving on to something else.

As I was further along in my career, opportunities that had been previously unavailable were presented to me. It was a gradual process. Incubating, unnoticed by me, was this accumulation of experiences.

These timely and fortuitous events unfurled at a point when I had the good fortune to be able to capitalize on them. Along with the spade work and the help of others to pull me along, there was a bit of good karma that struck at just the right moment.

8

Selling *Your* Talents to the Firm

DEVELOP A PLAN MANAGEMENT WILL LOVE

> "If we all did the things we are capable of doing, we would literally astound ourselves."[1]
>
> —Thomas Edison, American inventor (1847–1931)

Begin by looking at the world through the eyes of the firm when devising your negotiation strategy. The economic pie is only so big. Others need to have their portions cut thinner for the up-and-comers to enjoy a bigger slice. Younger partners can feel stifled waiting too long for an increased share of the profits, leading to talented attorneys departing for greener pastures. Freeing up some of the pie by reducing the compensation among the greying members of the firm is an exercise fraught with difficulties. However, this dynamic also opens the door for lawyers interested in slowing down. Offering assistance to the firm by suggesting your exit program creates more "pie" for younger partners will favorably attract the attention of management. That I guarantee.

Some of your partners will think you've lost your mind. Who offers to take a pay cut? As the year ends, those skeptics will be grinding it out, trying to make their billable hours goal. At the same time, you might be working a couple of days a week and otherwise hanging out with family, traveling, reading a book, taking that class you put off, or be retired altogether. You will have the last laugh once you cut your deal. You may even have a few jealous visitors sniffing around as they watch you enjoy

[1] QuotationsPage.com and Michael Moncur. "Quotations By Author: Thomas A. Edison (1847–1931)." Accessed April 26, 2023. http://www.quotationspage.com/quotes/Thomas_A._Edison/.

life. Don't be surprised if you have some lawyers you work with asking for your ideas to help them craft their exit arrangements. Be gracious.

I thought, then and now, that the program the firm and I constructed could be tweaked for other attorneys moving closer to the end of their careers. It can be difficult for a firm to entice every senior lawyer to buy into a one-size-fits-all-exit plan.

THIS PLAN WORKS IN SMALL FIRMS TOO

The notion that you can devise an exit strategy is not just for attorneys in big law firms. It may be simpler for small-firm practitioners to leave the law business. That's not to say it will be easy, but you begin with an advantage over big-firm lawyers of not having to negotiate your future with a management

Exercise #1
What's Your Bargaining Power?

List three things you offer to the firm that support you in getting what you want:

1.

2.

3.

team that may include lawyers you never even met. Lawyers in a small firm can create the same opportunities as practitioners toiling in other-sized operations. If you create the proper incentives, your younger lawyers will help finance your road to a different way of life. Transitioning management and client responsibilities to the up-and-comers means fewer hours in the office and more time for you to pursue leisure or other interests.

The principles for gliding out apply across the board. The skill you exhibited by developing your practice is what you are selling in your exit or wind-down agreement. Determine what you have brought to the table that makes you a valuable member of the firm. Then outline for your partner, or partners, how you will help the operation reap the benefits of your hard work as you slow down.

THE ADVANTAGE OF A SOLE PRACTITIONER

As a solo practitioner, you have built a practice that is an important asset—no need to close your shop and walk away. There is value in what you have created: with a proper plan, you can enjoy the fruits of your labor. Your options include selling your viable practice. You can ease your way toward the door by strategically grooming a younger lawyer to take over your book of business gradually.

It is important to plan for your day in the sun by making good hiring decisions 10 or more years before you plan to slow down or get out. Add a talented and ambitious young attorney to your letterhead. Spice your arrangement with a good faith promise that your new hire has the prospect of inheriting your firm (sort of).

Preparing for your exit requires more than employing sound hiring practices and solid mentoring. "Much of the value of the firm will lie in how it is organized, the stability it represents, and the repeat business your buyer will perceive as being available after the transaction,"[2] instructs attorney and author Gary Bauer. Simply hiring and retaining good lawyers is only part of the long-term preparation for using your law practice as a part of your retirement funding mechanism.

If you've made good hiring decisions and been a decent mentor, you've probably watched the development of your team. Be fair when it comes to

---

[2] Bauer, Gary P. *Hire and Retire—A Plan For A Continuing Income Stream In Retirement From Any Practice.* Chicago: ABA Book Publishing, 2019.

compensation. Be willing to take a pay cut to entice the next generation to send a few bucks your way as you slow down. This gesture is not an act of generosity. It is sound business judgment that will pay dividends in the form of loyalty and gratitude. Provide your young lawyers with the opportunity to thrive financially and professionally, and they will return the favor. It's a win-win.

Exercise #2
Starting the Process

List three things you need to do to start the process of negotiating your successful exit:

1.

2.

3.

I've seen it work very nicely for a senior, solo practitioner to join a firm at the end of a career. They introduced their clients to new lawyers and cut back their workload. I was always favorably impressed by what motivated these lawyers when vetting potential candidates with whom to ally. The primary concern was that the clients would be transitioned to good lawyers. The loyalty these lawyers exhibited to their clients was moving. They really cared.

I have seen it work the other way, as well. There are a lot of talented young lawyers out there. You probably run across a few of them every week in your practice. Not all of them want to practice in a large firm. Others may be looking for a new opportunity their smaller firm is not offering. Some lawyers—young and old—who would like to make a change don't always have the resources to hang a shingle. Scouting for someone to join a solo operation with the idea that he or she will, one day, take over your clients is not difficult. Your potential new associate, eventual partner, and the lawyer who may help finance your exit plan by purchasing your practice could be your adversary in one of your open files. Look across the table. There is no better way to evaluate a lawyer you wish to recruit for your firm than working on a deal or piece of litigation with them.

I spoke earlier about the growing pains that Dick and I experienced as our small law firm developed at the beginning of my practice. I didn't know it then but would one day learn that there are some anguish and restless moments at the other end of a lawyer's life, as well. It's the opposite of growing pains: I experienced some shrinking pains.

I was tossed a clue on the topic of the difficulty of getting out of the game in the early days of my career. I was amid negotiations in a case with a lawyer then in his 60s. We chatted as lawyers generally do whenever there was a lull in our conversation about the case. At that point in his career, Bill, my more senior lawyer friend, explained that he'd become more selective in what cases he accepted. This was a foreign concept to me at the time: turning down business. I was trying to build my practice. I would take on just about anything.

Bill was a golfer and enjoyed his leisure time. I asked him if he planned to stop taking on legal work altogether and retire to the golf course. I clearly remember his response, "McGoff, there's no easy way to get out of this business." Bill's observation made to me as a youngish lawyer 20-some years earlier turned out to be spot on. I've borrowed it many times.

BEWARE OF MISSION CREEP

Mission creep is a well-known affliction. It infects many facets of the practice of law. The cases we take on and projects within those cases often grow beyond our original expectations of what will be required. I'm sure you've quoted a fixed fee to a client, only to have underestimated the work it took to achieve your client's goal. I learned this lesson several times, the hard way. I tried a felony case twice, the second time pro bono because I neglected to account for how I would be paid should there be a mistrial. The law business, as you know, can be unpredictable.

Compensation-wise, all went well during the first three years of my arrangement. My pay and commitment to the firm were agreed upon. However, in the first two years of my sliding pay and diminishing hours commitment, I spent more hours than was agreed upon working for the firm. There was no history for this type of arrangement. It was an experiment. Given the inability to predict which crises might arise in any given year, it was impossible to accurately estimate how much time the general counsel (GC) position would require of me.

After the first year of this part of my arrangement, I didn't get too excited about going over the agreed-upon hours I worked. I liked what I was doing, the work was interesting, and it needed to be done. Of course, I requested some additional compensation. Some love? Perhaps a little bonus? How about some cash that says nice work to accompany the pat on the back? Nothing hit my bank account. I moved on a bit disgruntled but put it aside. I didn't have a meaningful conversation about resolving what I perceived to be an inequity.

When the same thing happened in year two, my feelings were a bit stronger. I had the same conversation with management as the year before. How about some acknowledgment other than a periodic "thank you, nice work" for a project well done? The inability to craft a solution to this mission creep was disappointing. I let it become aggravating and wasted too much energy complaining about it to others. I got some sympathy from the folks I whined to, but they could do nothing about it. I am now embarrassed that I griped so much to family, friends, and colleagues about a problem they could not solve. I weighed my options. Patty was tired of hearing me complain. The only way for me to be satisfied was to make it clear that I would no longer put in more hours than what my agreement stated.

TIME TO GO

When it came time to review my compensation at the beginning of 2018, I had determined that it would be my last year as GC. I made it clear that once I reached the agreed-upon hours' commitment, I would stop working as the GC no matter the date. I crafted a job description to be posted to find my replacement. It was ready in early spring. My idea was that the firm would put in place a new GC with whom I could work in the transition up to the end of the year.

It became evident in the spring that I was on track to put in the agreed-upon hours for which I was obligated by the end of the summer. September 1 looked to be the date when I would hit my hours commitment. I planned to then stop working as the GC. Though I had no desire to leave the firm in the lurch, I was not going to put in four months of work without compensation.

During the summer I met with various members of the firm's management to discuss compensation and the timing of my transition out of the firm. At the end of July, I sat down with some of those in positions of authority to express my intention to step down as GC when I had completed my commitment to the firm as GC for that year.

I was in the third year of my stepped-down hours and comp arrangement with the firm. Nearly seven months into 2018, I was close to putting in the hours required of me for the entire year. I reiterated that I was not going to put in more time than we had agreed upon as I had done the previous two years. I didn't expect the moon, but I figured that we could work out something satisfactory for both me and the firm.

When it became clear that we would not come to terms, I didn't miss the cue. I decided to aspire to a more leisurely day. I let the firm know that I'd be leaving my post as the firm's GC in about a month, the last day of August. It was a good decision.

Though I was briefly disappointed with how my active working days came to an end, I didn't dwell on it for long. I quickly embraced my newfound freedom. In fact, we took off for France for six weeks to commemorate it.

Exercise #3

What Are the Potential Pitfalls to Your Agreement?

List three things that could go wrong when you pitch your proposed new arrangement to firm management:

1.

2.

3.

PAPER IT UP

There are a few things to keep in mind as you prepare your strategy to leave the practice of law on your terms. Negotiating the provisions you would like with your law partners can get complicated. The old friend you've been practicing law with for 25 years, golfed with on the weekends, and saddled up to while having a toddy at the partners' retreats, well, their representative is now sitting across the bargaining table. Your interests and those of your partners may not be the same.

Executive coach for lawyers Anna Rappaport observes that "lawyers have skills around negotiations but they don't tend to bring them to the table when negotiating for their own careers."[3] Don't be bashful about getting professional advice. Sure, even when lawyers "lawyer up," people can get excited. You can discreetly solicit advice from a trusted lawyer if you wish to avoid the suggestion that you don't trust your law partners to deal with you fairly. However, no one should fault you for seeking professional advice if you elect to have counsel step forward and assist in papering up your deal. If anyone gives you grief about seeking counsel, ignore them. You shouldn't have any trouble identifying a qualified lawyer in whom you have the confidence to at least look over your shoulder before you ink your new deal with the firm.

While my agreement with the firm was in writing, there was one loose end. I should have included language that stated clearly how I would be compensated if I exceeded my hours' commitment during my final three years as GC. Likewise, the firm should have protected itself in the event that I duffed off and didn't show up as often as agreed. The GC—me—should have covered the firm in the event of this contingency. Had I solicited advice from any number of lawyer friends I could have retained to review and comment on my agreement, the disagreement I ended up having may have been avoided. I failed to follow the advice I had doled out many times in 40 years—talk to a lawyer.

If you are an owner of the firm and forfeiting that position is part of your wind-down arrangement, do so with caution. As a partner, the firm's operating agreement likely provides you with a lot of protection. Normally, it is difficult to remove an owner from the ranks. In some instances, the compensation of a partner cannot be dramatically reduced without good reason. Once you terminate your ownership interest and become an employee, any protection you may need should be set forth in your new agreement with the firm.

There were moments when my decision to give up my status as a partner appeared to be a mistake. At other times, it looked like a home run. Would I do it again? You bet! It set me on the path to making a change in my life. Of course, I'd have added a few tweaks to the agreement. As you evaluate your bargaining power and craft your way out the door, get some independent legal advice.

---

[3] Excelleration LLC. "About Anna Rappaport, Lawyer Coach." Accessed April 26, 2023. https://www.excellerationcoaching.com/anna-rappaport-lawyer-coach.

WHAT BEGAN WELL ENDED WELL

My professional career, like most winding roads, came with ruts and a few bumps. If I fell into a rut, I tried my best to get out quickly. I needed to slow down for the bumps. Navigated properly, they do little damage. I bounced out of the small ruts, steered around the bumps, and cruised toward the sunrise of a new life.

I had a good career. I was able to leave the law and do something else in life in part because of the opportunities that came my way at the law firm. The five years or so that I served as general counsel for my last law firm were among the most fulfilling in my career. My lawyer life had been pretty good.

There was another bright side to my decision to step down at age 65 that I had not anticipated when I negotiated my exit plan five years earlier. For several years, I had been systematically transferring my lawyer clients to a young partner. She had been working with me on ethics matters and attorney and judicial discipline cases for a long time. My phone was still ringing. Lawyers and others were asking for my advice or help with their legal predicaments. I knew my protégé was capable of taking good care of the clients I would leave behind, as well as those I was confident would come along in the future.

I also stepped aside from my role in a popular legal ethics program that I helped develop. The series of seminars, *Vignettes of Legal Ethics,* provided my primary marketing tool during the 25 years we presented. I met lawyers throughout Indiana and around the country through that seminar and the many others in which I participated. As part of my agreement to transition my business, I assisted the partner taking over my practice in taking my place on the dais, hoping that she would have a similar experience in enhancing her reputation as a lawyer's lawyer.

I reached an agreement with the firm for the last four months of 2018. A new GC was named. I agreed to assist the new GC as needed until the end of the year and would be paid hourly for my work. I would also receive a share of receipts for business I had put in the pipeline. The arrangement was fair and both parties benefited.

EXTENDING MY AGREEMENT

My phone was still ringing at the end of 2018. Former clients called looking for help. New clients also sought my assistance. Not wishing to dive back in, I passed on the business that came my way to lawyers in the firm.

I approached management and suggested that my fee-sharing arrangement be extended into the next year. It seemed like a win-win. Several of the young partners who were taking on the new work I was passing along advocated on my behalf. Another deal was struck. This arrangement worked well for me and the firm. I continued to share in receipts from clients I brought to the firm and several young partners added these clients to their book of business. The firm agreed to this arrangement for each of the next three years.

During that time, I helped with client matters when needed, which became less and less frequent. I decided not to get actively involved in any of the cases after the second year of the arrangement. My role with the firm evolved into mentoring younger lawyers and helping them develop their business by referring to them the clients still seeking my assistance.

Our financial plan was bolstered for several years by my continued stream of income. We didn't have to begin living solely off our retirement nest egg. During the last year and a half of my arrangement, I didn't bill an hour. We spent nine months in France waiting out COVID-19 in our small town. I was still taking calls and passing along business to the firm. Each month, the agreed-upon share of receipts generated by my book of business found its way to our bank account.

The firm benefited as I continued to bring in work. The young partners opened these new files and received billing credit that added to their numbers, making them happy. I enjoyed a stream of income that gradually diminished. It extended the glide path that I put in motion when I became GC. It helped me ease out of the law business gradually, which was my plan. The timeline of my slide out the door just became a little longer.

As I became less visible around the Indiana Bar, the frequency of calls naturally declined. I anticipated this would be the result of me spending less and less time in the office, at bar association programs, and being around other lawyers. Eventually, the amount of my monthly paycheck was less than I made on my paper route. I acted on this cue and asked the managing partner to meet me for lunch to discuss my future. At the end of 2021, I retired from the firm. Periodically I receive a call or an email from someone looking for my help on a matter or a referral. I'm happy to keep sending those matters to the talented lawyers that are still hard at work at my former law firm.

TALKING TO THE FIRM

Starting your conversation with those in charge is a momentous step. It's funny how difficult it is to talk about proposing a career change or retirement, even to partners who have been friends for many years. After spending years working together, making difficult decisions about the firm, managing complicated client matters together, and determining the careers of others, having a chat with our partners about our future makes us a nervous wreck.

Why is that? First, change is scary. It doesn't matter how smart or educated one is, taking the plunge into the unknown is daunting. It is also a step toward admitting that we've run our course. It's bittersweet to admit the end of a good thing is near. A big part of the uneasiness is the recognition of the chronology of life, our age. It's time to move on. Facing the fact that there are more years behind us than ahead isn't a comforting thought. It is difficult to admit. Telling the firm that age is part of the driving decision to slow down seems, well, a bit embarrassing. How'd I suddenly get to this point in life?

WHY IS THIS NOT SELLING?

When you speak with your partners about what you want to do, here's one dynamic you may experience. Professional executive coach Anna Rappaport described this phenomenon to me.

When you tell a partner, "I am thinking of retiring from the firm and pursuing other passions" or "I was thinking that I would like to take on a different role in the firm," there are two common reactions. The first reaction of the partner listening to your pitch may generally be about themselves. Common ones include:

- "I don't think I would be brave enough to try something like that."
- "I've always wanted to __________. Maybe I should try that."
- "Don't you think you will be bored?"
- "Do you really think that will work?"

In Anna's experience it is natural to compare oneself with other people, especially with people who are similarly situated to oneself. Such reactions are normal. The thing to remember is that the reaction is not about you. The partner may provide interesting information, ideas, or perspectives that can help you with your planning, but don't get sidetracked by their initial reactions. Whatever doubts they may share about the likelihood of your new arrangement failing or being untenable are more about themselves, their own self-confidence or perhaps lack thereof. Your personality, strengths, and resources may be very different from theirs. It is important to not be put off by other people's reactions.

The other common reaction, particularly among firm leaders, is about the impact on the firm. If you leave or change roles, what effect will that have on the finances of the firm, on the morale among partners and associates, or on the ability of the firm to retain your clients, among other concerns? Some people are more naturally resistant to change, while others are more flexible and open to engaging in brainstorming and exploring your proposal. If at first the reaction from firm leadership is negative, it may be because they are more resistant to change. Anna suggests that if you approach the discussions with persistence and focus on addressing their concerns, you are more likely to get what you want at the end of the day.

While you are dropping on management for the first time that you would like to move to part-time to be freed up to get your teaching license, the managing partner may be only half-listening. As you are making your pitch about why this is good for you and the firm, they are processing what you are telling them differently than you may expect.

Per Anna, it is natural for the recipient of a novel idea to put themselves into the other's shoes. It's human nature, she explained. As you make the ask, they begin an internal conversation while you are trying to sell your game plan. While you are talking, the managing partner may be thinking, "Wow, I'd like to do that. But dang, Nancy is in college, we just moved to that big house, and I want more in my retirement savings. I can't afford to cut back right now."

The managing partner's "Sorry, that is not going to work" response may be more about them than it is about you. Since going to part-time and taking a reduction in compensation is not going to work personally for the managing partner, they respond that it won't work for you or the firm.

Do not be too concerned if management's first reaction to your plan isn't gushingly supportive. If you've done your homework, circling back to the decision-makers will not be difficult. Let's face it, lawyers are a cautious bunch. We're not always quick to change. The new and the novel need to be properly vetted. Don't let an initial skeptical reaction to your idea be discouraging.

Here's another negotiating tip Anna shared with me. It's not a good idea to spring your plan to change your career path on the management team. Approach each of the decision-makers one at a time. It's likely that you know them, maybe some of them well. You will be able to more fully explain how modifying your career path benefits the firm over several one-on-one lunches. Fifteen minutes on the management committee's monthly agenda is not enough time to make a proper pitch for your future. As you learned in Politics 101, know the vote count before the vote is counted.

WHAT'S HOLDING US BACK

So why do we hesitate to talk about a plan that will enrich our lives with decision-makers? That's a tough question with no easy answer. The reluctance to declare to our firm it is time for us to move on is not an uncommon phenomenon. After spending a professional life building a career and to now state publicly it is time to give it up is a hard road to cross. There's the obvious fear of rejection. What if this announcement is seen as a sign of weakness and an opportunity for management to put one out to pasture on the firm's terms? I could go on listing potential sources of angst for you. Instead, I want to point you to a resource that may provide solace and inspiration, as well as food for thought.

There is a recent addition to the literature aimed at those contemplating making a life change. Author and Harvard Professor Arthur Brooks' thoughtful book, *Strength to Strength: Finding Happiness and Deep Purpose In The Second Half Of Life,*[4] is a fitting addition to the shelf of the curious professional's library.

Brooks writes of the need "to let go of some things in your life that you worked hard for—but that are now holding you back. To adopt parts of life that will make you happy, even if they don't make you special."

What gives one pause at the moment just before declaring we plan to embark on a new adventure is personal. We each harbor our own set of fears. However, a big part of the reluctance to tell our partners we are moving on is ego. letting go of it, that is. It's a topic worth spending some time contemplating.

---

[4] Brooks, Arthur C. *Strength to Strength: Finding Success, Happiness, and Deep Purpose In The Second Half Of Life*. New York: Portfolio, 2022

DO THE RIGHT THING OR BEWARE YOUR AUDIENCE

I provided ethics advice to lawyers throughout most of my career. The instinct to pause and consider if there are ethical implications to a course of action is still in the blood. Talking about planning an exit from a lawyering life, or a change in careers had me dusting off my GC thinking cap. I followed my old advice and consulted an expert in the field, Cari Sheehan, a professor of business law and ethics at Indiana University. She also has experience working in the office of general counsel of a national law firm.

Here's one ethics pothole in your road to a new life as you share your retirement musings with certain lawyer friends. Let's start with this straightforward concept that Sheehan laid out when I spoke with her. "It is well established under ethical principles that all partners, associates, and employees (whether legal or nonlegal) owe duties of loyalty to the firm in which they work. This means more than just avoiding conflicts of interest and following the firm's policies. It may mean that there is an obligation to alert the firm of things that may be adverse to the firm's interest."

Most of us have been exposed to partners who checked out. I call it retiring in place. Perhaps their practice dried up due to a change in the industry they served or a merger by which the client's GC or manager who was feeding them business was replaced. There could be lots of reasons but the bottom line is they no longer contribute to the partnership's coffers as in the old days. However, they come to the office every day and remain a partner. In more extreme cases, the lawyer retreats to a sunny vacation home and rarely darkens the firm's corridors.

In my experience, partners are loathe to boot out other partners, particularly when they have been with the firm a long time. It seems unsavory and it is complicated. Often the construct of the partnership agreement allows for those retiring in place to glide down the economic scale gracefully over some years.

Whatever you call it, the early years of this type of retirement are funded by the other partners. That's not cool. However, it happens and it is no secret while it is happening.

With that backdrop and the professor's brief ethics lesson, let's get back to your discussion with the firm. When kicking around ideas about how to retire or reduce your commitment with the firm, the conversations mostly, but not always, start with family. However, lawyers gravitate to lawyers and ultimately we tend to test our ideas on those lawyers we are closest to. Many times, we are closest to those we spend most of our waking hours with during the course of our career: our law partners.

When hashing out options with one of your partners, it would be unwise to muse about retiring in place or some other alternative that is not beneficial to the firm if the proposal you've crafted for your next act is not accepted by the firm. It would also be unfair to your partners. Thinking out loud or brainstorming the retirement in place alternative risks compromising your long-time colleague. It's clearly not in the firm's best interest for a partner to retire in place.

I would not recommend hardball tactics when negotiating an exit plan. That is not the time and place. Suggesting to your best friend and law partner that you may retire in place or employ some other device that is not in the firm's best interest to get your way is a bad idea. Doing so presents them with the difficult choice of reporting your actions to management or shirking their fiduciary responsibility to the firm in deference to your friendship.

Of course, the easy way to avoid this issue is to stay on a higher road. You cannot expect to get everything you want in your deal with the firm. I've never been a big fan of using a threat as a negotiating strategy. However, if you plan to wax on about a retirement plan that is not in the firm's best interest, don't do it with a law partner.

BE BOLD, NOT CRAZY

Don't sell yourself short by underestimating your value to the operation. One point to consider is the current fluidity within the legal marketplace. It's no secret that law firms are sometimes challenged when it comes to devising exit plans for their senior lawyers. This creates an open door for the creative lawyer who brings to management's table an idea that suits the lawyer's future plans as well as the law firm. Lawyers with good practices changing firms near the end of their careers have become more common. These departing partners sometimes pocket a signing bonus as part of the package. That, I promise, has not gone unnoticed by firm management teams. Be bold but not crazy when laying out your ideas on how to ratchet down your career to your managing partner. If you are a partner, they can't fire you, right? You may have other options if you don't find a willingness to help you create the plan you desire.

Often, when the firm would like to see a lawyer transition, those who have been at it for years are not ready to let go of their clients, their status as a partner, and the money that goes with it. When management comes knocking to discuss a lawyer's exit strategy, the visit is sometimes poorly received. Perhaps they are not ready to transition from "who's who to who's he?" discussed in Arthur Brooks' book, *Strength to Strength.*[5] However, if you are willing to start reducing your income along with your time in the office, this creates an opportunity. There is no point in waiting for the managing partner to show up in your office with the firm's transition plan.

I believed that I had bargaining power when I approached the firm's management with my proposal to ease out of the practice of law. I'll bet you do, as well. I had a good business developed during 30-plus years. I was training a young partner to step in and take over my book of business. Clients were accepting this transition without pushback. The firm needed to have a general counsel, and I had the background and experience to fill this need. I also demonstrated a willingness to give on two things in exchange for crafting the deal I wanted: I would relinquish my partnership and I was willing to reduce my compensation. Be willing to give up something to make your proposal sellable.

Evaluate your book of business as a part of your game plan. What will it look like in 10 years? If your plan is to make a move earlier, what is your assessment of the ability to attract and retain clients over the next three to five years? You likely have other talents that you've brought to the firm aside from the client side of this business. In a larger firm, skills as a mentor or being a sounding board for management ought not to be overlooked. Act boldly and proceed with confidence. You are likely to discover as Thoreau observed that "if one advances confidently in the direction of his dreams, and endeavors to live the life which he has imagined, he will meet with a success unexpected in common hours."[6]

My endgame worked out better than planned. There is no reason you can't enjoy a similar experience. When you are prepared to move along

---

[5] Brooks, Arthur C. *Strength to Strength: Finding Success, Happiness, and Deep Purpose In The Second Half Of Life*. New York: Portfolio, 2022.

[6] Thoreau, Henry David. *Walden; or, Life in the Woods*. Boston: Ticknor and Fields, 1854.

in your life, don't underestimate your bargaining power. Do you like your office where it is right now? Would you like to begin spending more time away from that office without moving your desk down the street to another law firm? If so, identify the person you are closest to in your firm's management. Construct an exit plan that suits you. Make sure there is something in it for your firm. Vet it with the person in your life that will benefit by you being around the house more. Show your plan to a trusted colleague. Talk to a lawyer. Then walk down the hall, use your lawyer skills for yourself and sell it to the firm. It's your turn.

MEETING WITH THE BOSS

A friend shared with me how he prepared for the big talk about retirement with our law firm's management. The closer he came to the decision to declare his exit date, the more frequently he vetted his plan with his wife. In the evenings over a glass of wine on the back porch, they kicked around ideas of what life would be like without the chains of billable hours, partner's meetings, and client demands. He outlined what his talk with the managing partner would sound like. It was a good exercise. They were both excited and ready for the next chapter. One night the session ended with resolve. They clinked their glasses and made a toast to their future. Tomorrow would be the day.

My friend had toiled in the firm for more than 30 years. He'd served in various management capacities. This trusted partner was on good terms and had worked closely with the managing team for many years. But the next morning when the moment came to go down the hall and share his plans with the managing partner, he paused. The bravado exuded during the practice run with his spouse the previous evening could not be mustered. Suddenly, he was second-guessing his decision. As he walked toward the managing partner's office, turning around in his head was, "Maybe this can wait after all. No need to do it today. Perhaps I need to tweak my plan before starting this discussion."

This, of course, put him between a rock and a hard place. If he didn't have the talk, he'd have to go home and tell his wife he chickened out. Twelve hours earlier he was telling her how he'd resolved to announce to the firm his plan to slow down and spend more time at home.

He had the talk, but not before this last-minute panic about having a conversation with his friend and long-time colleague who was the managing partner. We had a good laugh about how difficult it was to step into the boss's office and talk about winding down his career, after it sounded so easy the night before when plotting it from the safety of his own backyard.

His experience was by no means unique. The path to the managing partner's office to have the talk may seem like walking the plank. Announcing that you've decided to slow down or retire after a long career takes courage.

9

Funding Your Next Stage

It's not my intent to help you craft a financial plan. That's not my expertise. However, it occurred to me when mapping out this book that there is no way to avoid touching on the topic of money when discussing your future. What you accumulate for your nest egg and what you spend necessarily factor into your planning. Though things will change along the way for any number of reasons, grasping the nuts and bolts of your personal finances is a must. The sooner you jump on this project, the better.

> "An education isn't how much you have committed to memory, or even how much you know. It's being able to differentiate between what you know and what you don't."[1]
>
> —Anatole France, French poet, journalist, and novelist (1844–1924)

I learned a few things along the way that I wish to share with you. The most important thing is: don't be discouraged by the belief that you'll never have the resources to retire, change careers, or keep your day job but work at a slower pace. In my very early days of lawyering, I left meetings with our financial advisor wondering how I got myself into a position requiring a King Midas-sized pile of gold to step back from work. Over time we became more sophisticated clients of our financial advisors. Once we developed a personalized plan, the takeaway from these meetings started to become more encouraging. In this chapter, I want to dispel the myth that you have to be wealthy to transition to a new life.

1 BrainyQuote. "Anatole France Quotes." Accessed April 26, 2023. https://www.brainyquote.com/quotes/anatole_france_101422.

There were three simple points that, once I understood their collective impact, opened my eyes to how I could move on. Applied together, they pushed me to a comfort zone where I was convinced that I could reduce the hours I was working, take the corresponding pay cut, and begin to live a better life. There is nothing earth-shattering about any one of these points. Realizing them took some discipline, and that didn't happen overnight. You need to:

1. Know what you spend
2. Devise a savings plan
3. Develop a strategy for eliminating debt

That's it—nothing new here. You've heard this before. Employed collectively, you will achieve your goals.

Let's be realistic. You can't put this book down and sketch out how to finance your next phase of life in an hour. That exercise will take some time. It will require research, critical thought, and, most likely, the input of a professional. The plan here is to introduce you to a few concepts to get you started.

If you begin by thinking about what you wish to be doing after you stop lawyering and before you acquire more grey hair, your interests are likely to change. The dream of buying a sailboat and scuba diving in the Caribbean may give way to a newfound passion for snow skiing. A place in the mountains will then be better suited for you. Perhaps those ideas will one day change to simply moving into a smaller home and spending time volunteering, watching grandchildren's soccer matches, and watering your garden. You will continually tweak your financial plan as your plans for your future life become clearer.

TAKE ADVANTAGE OF AVAILABLE RESOURCES

Patty and I long ago began to rely on professionals to guide us toward our financial goals. Our initiation into retirement planning occurred when I was in my 30s, and it was by happenstance.

I practiced law and managed my business. Patty cut hair and ran her salon. After 10 years of marriage, we added raising 3 children to our daily schedules. Micromanaging our finances was not within either of our skill sets nor were we interested in adding more to our plates by educating ourselves in the field of money management. That's not to suggest that we didn't pay attention to our finances. Early on, we devised a savings plan for the year, which mostly consisted of trying to max out our retirement savings. This was accomplished during a brief chat in which we identified our spending and savings goals, and then we went about our lives. As our kids began to leave home and our interest in changing our lifestyle grew stronger, we paid more attention to our savings. We also met with our advisor more frequently.

We identified what we didn't know. Crafting a financial plan wasn't an exercise either of us was trained to lead. We identified experts engaged in the full-time business of financial planning and sought their advice. Along the path, we changed advisors several times when we found a better fit for where we were at that point in our lives.

FINDING A FINANCIAL ADVISOR

Patty and I met our current financial advisor in a roundabout way. In the early 1980s, the 10-lawyer firm in which I was an associate started a retirement program where it matched our contributions. At around age 30, I began putting away money for retirement. The advisor who set up the plan gave us pointers on where to invest our first few bucks as we had no clue. At some point, I reconnected with a high school friend who was an advisor at a large brokerage firm. We began working with him until he was promoted and moved on, at which time we worked with another advisor at the firm.

After my father-in-law retired, Bill carefully tracked the few stocks he traded. When not devising a contraption to keep the squirrels off his birdfeeder, the ups and downs of his portfolio were cataloged daily in a tiny notebook he kept in the kitchen. Bill was a saver, having grown up during the Great Depression. His 40 years' worth of working days were spent in a machine shop making bearings for automobiles. At some point, a young financial advisor, Michael Wright, knocked on my in-laws' door. At that time, door-knocking was how some financial advisors got started. Michael asked if my in-laws would consider investing with his firm, to which they agreed. Bill then had the advisor's professionally produced monthly reports to supplement the tracking of his investments in his miniature notebook.

When Patty's mother died in 2002, she left a little dough to Patty and her siblings. The money was in the account that Michael had established. He had been managing it for Patty's mom during the years after Bill passed away. Patty met with Michael. She liked him and appreciated the program he had established for her parents. She decided to leave the funds in the account she inherited. It was no fortune but was a nice contribution to our investment account that was being neglected in favor of college tuition payments.

Eventually, we decided to place some of our funds with Michael. We wanted to do a test run to determine if making a change in investment advisors was wise. After a few years, we found that Michael fit our needs as an advisor. We moved our accounts. You could say we met our financial advisor through Patty's dad, although Bill had passed away and was not here to make a formal introduction.

Our financial advisor became our partner in planning early in the relationship. We were not interested in hot stock tips or ideas for a big score. We expected that we would develop a plan that resulted in having sufficient resources to pay our bills, educate our kids, and, one day, retire. I never thought of us as investors. We were planners. Everyone is different, though. There are qualified advisors out there to suit investors, planners, and those risk-takers looking for a frequent windfall from a stock sold after it skyrockets in value.

WE HAVE MET THE ENEMY AND IT IS US

Procrastination may be practiced at many levels. Perhaps your to-do list bears no red slashes through completed tasks. So what, you say? "I can knock off a few of those urgencies before noon." Or maybe "I'll get on it tomorrow. It will be here soon enough." Ever been caught short by thinking, "That project will not take all that long; it's not due till next Friday. I'll get on it next Thursday."? I've used all these excuses. Sometimes I discovered that what I put off to the last minute required more work to complete than I had time to get it done.

Most, if not all of us, are procrastinators of sorts. It's a matter of degrees. For some, procrastination is a way of life, an art form. Procrastination can be a temporary affliction for others, their attention briefly diverted by a walk, a few chapters of a good book, or a night off with a movie. Then they are back on task in the morning, getting it done.

Paying attention to the details of your financial plan cannot begin too soon. This is a slice of life not to be put on the back burner. Even master procrastinators must make an exception and turn their attention to their personal or family balance sheet from time to time. There is no reason to be consumed by money talk, spreadsheets, and checking your phone every hour of the day to see whether the DOW, NASDAQ, or S&P 500 sank or soared. Taking your financial pulse on a regular basis will move you forward toward your goals, but you don't need to be obsessed with it.

OPENING MOVES

If you are already working with someone, good for you. I'm not suggesting that anyone change horses. There is no reason to interfere with your established relationship with a financial advisor. If you are a "do-it-yourself" type, there's a mountain of resources out there for you. If you fall into the camp of folks looking for a financial advisor, though, there are a few basic questions that you will want to answer for yourself so that you can get started.

These are big-picture concepts. You will need to carefully think about each of them. I suggest that you get pen and paper in hand—or fire up your computer—and do some work. You will revisit these points many times as you progress toward the date you plan to change gears. As you become better educated about your finances and begin to hone in on what you genuinely want to do with your life, your answers to these questions will change.

You could attempt a first draft as you gather the information to answer the questions. However, if you are like me, you may need some help to come up with the correct answers to these seemingly simple questions.

Exercise #1
Three Basic Questions to Ask Yourself

---

1. How much is enough?

2. What economic resources do I truly need to shift gears, change jobs, transition to another phase of life, or simply retire? In other words: what do I spend?

3. If you are fortunate to, at some point, have sufficient resources to care for yourself and your loved one, what is the purpose of any money that exceeds what you need?

HOW MUCH IS ENOUGH?

"If you die with too much money, you worked too long." We've been working with our financial advisor for 20 years now. Michael has dropped this phrase on us more than a few times. Though said in jest, there's always been more than a kernel of truth for Patty and me in his quip.

If you could choose the day of your departure from this planet, this question would be much easier to answer. But you can't. This means there will necessarily be some guesswork here. There are many planning tools available to help you answer the "how-much-do-I-need" question, but it will always be a tad speculative.

To find your answer, you are going to have to do a bit of soul-searching, reflecting on what it is you are truly working toward. Working backward is a good exercise. What is the purpose for your monetary resources that exceed what you need beginning on the day when you're not around? Should you leave a legacy to your children, educate the grandchildren, or donate to a worthy charity? Perhaps you plan to die with no will and let the relatives squabble over your estate, enriching some lawyers in the process. There are many more possible uses for your excess resources than you may think of as you contemplate this question.

Generic financial planning calculators—there are numerous available online—can be a great place to start your self-education into your financial future. But beware. Do not be discouraged by the numbers these templates may throw out. The results could make retirement appear to be a daunting, if not impossible, task. However, you may find that you are closer to hitting your number than you thought. If your estate plan is to spend what you have earned and saved for your transition and/or retirement—not worrying about leaving a legacy—your "I'm-finished" number may not appear so daunting.

If you are serious about planning for your future, you need to customize the financial calculator. It needs to be personalized, particularly when contemplating future spending. What you spend will be key to determining whether you risk outliving your resources. Only with a personalized plan can you identify the target date for your landing zone. The best way to develop a personalized financial plan is to bring on board a professional to assist you.

WHAT DO YOU SPEND?

The best way to figure out what it will take to permanently hang up your court-going suits is to determine what you may spend, not how much money you will have in the bank. Sure, you must have resources, but your spending will determine on what day you can walk away. It's the spending piece that can also lead to frustration if you don't take command of your financial planning and insist on having it personalized. Generic retirement calculators are not set up to account for how people actually spend in retirement. Getting the spending metric right is what got me to my landing zone faster than I, at one time, believed would be possible.

Incredibly, it took us three years to nail down the answer to the simple question: "How much do we spend?" First, we had to come up with a template for expenses. The next step was to begin to monitor our monthly expenses. We tracked them for another three or four years. Only then were we comfortable that we had a firm handle on what it really costs to manage our household, educate our kids, and otherwise live our lives.

Not everyone needs to undertake this exercise today. Maybe you'd like to satisfy your curiosity and see where your money is going. Whether you want or need to engage in this tedious task may depend upon your current stage in your career, your age, and the target date for your exit. If you are like us—at the stage in life when we were paying a mortgage, plus education costs, soccer, gymnastics, and volleyball club fees—you are investing little to no time evaluating your expenses. Our financial analysis at that point was no deeper than, "How much is in the checking account?" "How much will be coming in before the bills are due?" And, "Can we afford this?" There was no deep dive. Patty and I weren't analyzing and tracking spending. We were busy raising our family. For many years, we were on a "pay-as-we-go" plan.

When I first began to think of changing gears, Patty and I could only give a general answer to the question "What do we spend?" It was only when we became serious about the idea of me cutting back on work and perhaps transitioning into another way of life that we began to look critically at our spending. That was around the spring of 2007 when I was 54 years old and Patty was 52. We had a senior in high school, our son was soon to graduate from Indiana University, and our other daughter was a sophomore at Regis University. We were looking at two expensive years with both girls attending a Jesuit college in Denver. We had a total of six more years of college to pay, but we would be done in the spring of 2011. Though it sounds a bit reckless, we were married for 36 years before we began to work on understanding our expenses.

Now, it's easy for me to say that the exercise of determining your spending is not that difficult. Patty is the bookkeeper. She uses a Quicken program and catalogs our expenses every month. It's a time-consuming endeavor for her. My suggestion that we hold our monthly review is not always met with the same enthusiasm as proposing that we go out for dinner. Unless you are incredibly frugal, sitting on some millions, or both, deciding to cut off an income stream to which you have become accustomed is a daunting step in your life. You better know how much you spend before you walk away from your paycheck or monthly draw.

WHAT IS YOUR SPENDING TARGET?

I run when I hear the word budget. Patty is even quicker to find a way to end the discussion when this word is in the mix. I suggest not thinking about a "budget." Let's talk about your "spending target." Determine your spending goal for the next 12 months. We have found that using the calendar year makes it easier but do not delay this exercise until New Year's Day. Get started now. Your spending target will largely be dictated by your existing bills. Unless you have a forgiving lender, your mortgage payment is not optional. Many of you, I suspect, have a system for tracking expenses in place.

Appendix B provides our spending template that you may find useful to determine the information you need to complete the first step of creating your financial plan.

Exercise #2
What is Your Spending Target?

1. How much do you currently spend? (Make a list of what you spend and how you spend it. Leave nothing out.)

2. How can you adjust your spending to ensure more retirement savings?

3. What are your most expensive debts?

4. What can you do to get rid of them?

FUNDING RETIREMENT VIA INHERITANCE

I have no firsthand experience being the beneficiary of a sizeable inheritance. If only we could all be so fortunate. I have often used the well-worn quip, "He or she made their money the old-fashioned way—it was inherited."

I have joked with my brothers that Mom and Dad could have done us the favor of being a Vanderbilt or Rothschild. I could have forgone the working life of a lawyer, writing down my time in 10th-of-an-hour increments for nearly 40 years. My brother John would not have had his sleep pattern disrupted by pulling 30 years' worth of all-night shifts as an emergency room physician. My brother Jim, a lawyer/accountant, would not have had to endure six-hour round trips to the toll road to check on the toll booths as a part of his role in supervising the system. My sister Patty's out-of-state tuition payments for her boys to attend university would not have required her to go back to work, and our brother Terry could have spent Saturdays at home instead of minding his auto parts store. Our sister Mary Therese, on the other hand, took a different path. She is not idle by any means, but as a member of a religious community, she leads a more contemplative life.

Alas, we were dropped at birth into a different zip code. The truth is that few of us would trade our lives. No one in my family is complaining, but the occasional daydream about what a lottery jackpot would have done for us or how a trust fund from which to draw may have made things different is not out of line. It's okay to wonder "what if?" but unless you are certain that you will inherit your retirement resources, you need to stop dreaming and start planning.

A WORD ABOUT HEALTHCARE

As with every element of your retirement planning, healthcare needs are personal. I'm no expert on Medicare or the field of health insurance. However, over the years, we were covered by my law firm's healthcare plans. I've evaluated our family's health insurance plans throughout my working days. Ultimately, and with assistance, we figured out the Medicare maze before I hit 65.

There are experts out there to help you navigate the choppy waters of our country's inexplicably complicated health insurance system. If your eyes gloss over as you try to figure out what health plan is best for you, contact someone who does this for a living. Even if trying to unravel the various options doesn't put you to sleep, speak with an expert. That's what

Patty and I did, and we're very satisfied with where we ultimately landed. Let me share a few thoughts on the topic.

I want to begin by telling you that there are some scaremongers out there. As you research the topic of how to pay for healthcare in retirement, there are some whopping numbers put up by some studies. The crowd that suggests you better keep working if you don't have a fortune in the bank is at work when it comes to predicting the cost of your future health care. For example, in 2021 Fidelity Investments' 20th Annual Retiree Health Cost Estimate report publicized that a 65-year-old couple may expect to spend $300,000 on healthcare in retirement.[2] These numbers used to send me into the doldrums. It was just one more pile of cash I didn't have that must be set aside if I want to walk away from the law business and not spend my life stressing over future medical bills. I want to encourage you: future health-care costs are manageable. Make this subject a part of your dialogue as you construct your plan.

A 2015 survey reported that almost 75 percent of those responding said that being able to afford health care in retirement was a concern. My take-away from that scary statistic is simple. Folks need to understand how the system works, get direction from someone who knows what they are talking about, and then plan accordingly. Done properly, the concern that you won't have the resources to pay your doctor can be alleviated.

For starters, you have more flexibility now than you had in the past. More than 70 percent of Americans are covered to some extent by an employer-sponsored health insurance program.[3] In the past, the need to maintain health insurance tied many to jobs they wanted to quit. The rules were changed, allowing workers to switch jobs without fear of losing their health insurance. However, it wasn't long ago that people were forced

---

[2] Tessier, Michelle. "Fidelity's 20th Annual Retiree Health Care Cost Estimate Hits New High: A Couple Retiring Today Will Need $300,000 to Cover Medical Expenses, an 88% Increase Since 2002." Fidelity. May 07, 2021. https://newsroom.fidelity.com/pressreleases/fidelity-s-20th-annual-retiree-health-care-cost-estimate-hits-new-high-a-couple-retiring-today-will/s/e76142b7-7efa-4b76-a49d-f96791ad3dd0.

[3] Spiegel, Jake and Paul Fronstin. "What Employers Say About the Future of Employer-Sponsored Health Insurance." Commonwealth Fund. January 26, 2023. https://www.commonwealthfund.org/publications/issue-briefs/2023/jan/what-employers-say future-employer-health-insurance#:~:text=Today%2C%20employer%2Dsponsored%20insurance%20represents,(see%20the%20exhibit%20below).

to stay in employment positions they loathed because leaving their job meant theirs, or a family member's, pre-existing medical condition would be excluded from coverage by their new employer's policy. Talk about being handcuffed to your job.

This unfair practice was legislated out of existence as a part of the Affordable Care Act in 2014. Now there's not only more flexibility, but there are also more ways for a self-employed person or one taking retirement before age 65 to be insured. Maintaining a suitable health insurance plan no longer must lock one into an undesirable job.

The cost of health insurance or calculating one's Medicare premiums is not complicated. However, our overall health, the medications we take, and the number of doctor visits in any given year are individualized variables. Consequently, what we each will need to spend to maintain our health will greatly vary.

It was reported in *The Retirement Management Journal* that the average annual spend on healthcare, excluding long-term care, for the 65 to 94 age group is about $4,500 per person.[4] That includes premiums and out-of-pocket costs. Patty and I are spending more, around $15,000 a year. Our out-of-pocket costs during my last year as a partner in the firm were north of $18,000. I recently heard of a partner leaving the firm for an in-house position with better benefits. As a law firm partner, he was paying $25,000 per year for insurance and copays for a family of four.

Don't stress about the fantastical numbers some suggest you'll need to pay your doctors and dentists in your dotage. Put an expert on your team that traffics in health insurance for the self-employed or retirees. Your future healthcare should not be a roadblock to your successful transition to life after lawyering.

YOUR MONTHLY CHECK IN RETIREMENT

Most of us have been paying into the Social Security Administration (SSA) our entire working lives. I first paid into the system in 1969, according to the annual statement I receive from SSA. I pulled in $179 that year working

4 Halen, Nick, Kelli Faust, and Todd Taylor. "Understanding the True Cost of Health Care in Retirement." *Retirement Management Journal* 9, No. 1 (2020): 52. https://investmentsandwealth.org/getattachment/96f59ebb-d287-4be5-a081-3e3b4a8e63ba/RMJ091-TrueCostOfHealthCareinRetirement.pdf.

in the kitchen at Mr. D's Restaurant. Other than in 1977, when my gross income was $24, my paychecks, fortunately, increased after my chicken cutting days in the restaurant.

If you've not already done so, you should set up your online SSA account. *My Social Security* is easily accessed at https://www.ssa.gov/. There is a lot of good information on the site, and it will be essential to your planning. Once you are set up in the system, the information available to you is individualized. You will be able to see what your actual anticipated benefit will be depending upon what age you begin to draw your check. This number will be essential as you decide on what date you'd like to leave the office for the last time.

You know that social security is funded by a payroll tax on wages. It was implemented in the 1930s when President Franklin D. Roosevelt's (FDR) administration initiated the concept of old-age financial security and unemployment benefits. FDR made it clear that we would reap the benefits of our contributions into the system. "We put those payroll contributions there to give the contributors a legal, moral, and political right to collect their pensions and their unemployment benefits. With those taxes in there, no damn politician can ever scrap my social security program."[5] I've never bought into the notion that the social security system is going bust, nor that our benefits are at risk of not being paid. There are some that may disagree. I've chosen not to waste much time on the periodic articles in the news predicting what I believe to be an unlikely doomsday event.

I believe that FDR's observation, made in 1941, was spot on. You can bet that we included our anticipated income from social security in our earliest financial plans. The program is too popular for Congress to simply eliminate it. Plus, it's our money; we paid into the program. I believe it will continue to provide an income stream for us, for you, and others entitled to it down the road. Imagine the political backlash if there was ever a serious effort to rob you and the rest of the working public of your "legal, moral, and political right" to collect the money *you* invested in the plan. Sure, the program will be tweaked again and again, but I've never worried about our social security checks drying up, nor should you.

---

[5] FDR said this to Luther Gluck who recorded it in a memo. This quote comes from the Social Security Administration's Historian recounting the story and reproducing Gluck's memo. See more at https://www.ssa.gov/history/Gulick.html.

YOU NEED A FINANCIAL VISION

There is no escaping the fact that having a financial vision must be a part of your planning. There's no way around it. Grasping the handle on your expenses, which is not always an easy task, is a first step. Don't be discouraged if it takes time to bring your spending into clear focus. It took Patty and me several years. That was after living about 35 years of our married lives on the spend-as-you-go plan.

Educating yourself on the other resources that will be at your disposal should bring you comfort. You will get a pension check every month in the form of your social security benefit. Your monthly check may not be sufficient to live on, but it will pay some bills.

Healthcare is going to be covered by Medicare. Of course, there will be medical expenses that you pay out of pocket, but you may find this health insurance system less expensive than what you've been accustomed to as a working lawyer.

There is work for you to do to set yourself up for the next financial phase of your life. You will have help in the form of benefits that you earned during your working days. The next chapter will also help you to figure out what is your level of comfort regarding your future finances.

THERE IS NO SUCH THING AS EASY MONEY: THE OLD WOMAN VS. THE FRENCH LAWYER

One of my favorite stories about the fiction of easy money involves a Frenchwoman and a lawyer in the town of Arles in the south of France. Arles was an important town when the Romans occupied that part of the world. The amphitheater in the town's center, constructed around 90 AD, is still being used. Those interested in art will associate Arles with Vincent van Gogh. Today you can visit sites and structures where he painted when living there in the late 19th century.

Jeanne Calment was born in Arles in 1875. While working in her grandfather's shop as a teenager, she sold art supplies to van Gogh. In 1965, the then 90-year-old Madame Calment sold her apartment in Arles to a 45-year-old lawyer, Francois Raffray, using a vehicle called a *viager*.

Real estate transfers *en viager* make up a small portion of French real estate transactions. The term means "life annuity." This system has been on the books in France since 876 AD. The purchaser in a *viager* transaction pays a reduced price for a home. The seller remains in the residence and receives from the buyer an agreed-upon monthly fee for the duration of the seller's life.

The buyer gambles on the seller's lifespan. The shorter the seller's time on earth after inking the deal, the better the buyer's investment. The sellers augment their pensions with the cash payment and the monthly stipend. Sounds like a win-win. What could possibly go wrong? Let me tell you.

After paying the agreed-upon purchase price, Monsieur Raffray was obligated to pay Madame Calment 2,500 francs per month, about $500 at the time. Unfortunately for Monsieur Raffray, Madame went on to be the world's oldest living person. She passed away at the age of 122, 32 years after striking her *viager* agreement with lawyer Monsieur Raffray.

As for Monsieur Raffray, he died two years before Madame Calment. His family was obligated to continue to pay the 2,500-franc monthly stipend after his death. It was reported in the *New York Times* that Madame Calment enjoyed a meal of foie gras, duck thighs, cheese, and chocolate cake on her 120th birthday. At the time, she was living in a nursing home, not in the apartment that the Raffray family was waiting to take charge of. Madame Calment made a good deal. She collected more than twice the value of the apartment. As for Monsieur Raffray, to quote Madame Calment, "In life, one sometimes makes bad deals."[6]

---

[6] The Associated Press. "A 120-Year Lease on Life Outlasts Apartment Heir." *The New York Times*. December 29, 1995. https://www.nytimes.com/1995/12/29/world/a-120-year-lease-on-life-outlasts-apartment-heir.html; .https://www.bbc.com/news/magazine-33326787.

10

Calculating Your Realistic Financial Needs

> "For many people, being asked to solve their own retirement savings problems is like being asked to build their own cars."[1]
>
> —Richard Thaler, American economist

You need to have the confidence that your financial plan will carry you into your next endeavor. Once you make the leap, it may not be easy to return to where you've been. The day after your office is cleaned out, a new tenant will be moving in to enjoy the view. It may be impossible to reverse the reduction in billable hours you negotiated. You only want to ratchet back up your obligation to the firm because you wish to do so—not because you have to.

A professional can guide you to the number it takes for you to breathe easily. You don't want to spend your newfound life staring at your monthly bank and brokerage account statements, fearing you will run out of resources. The financial peace of mind to go about your business without looking back, fearing you cut off or reduced your revenue stream too soon, can be attained. Let me share my thoughts on how to get there.

Do you believe that at age 81, you will be windsurfing in the Caribbean, hiking down the Grand Canyon, or bungee jumping in Belize? Do you think your expenses will go down as you get into later retirement years? Most of us will slow down as we age, and our spending will slow down with us.

There are outliers, of course. There are seniors who have run marathons and some who have sky-dived after their 90th birthday. It's not

1 Thaler, Richard. "Shifting Our Retirement Savings Into Automatic." *The New York Times*, April 6, 2013. https://www.nytimes.com/2013/04/07/business/an-automatic-solution-for-the-retirement-savings-problem.html.

unusual for golfers who have reached the century mark to play 18 holes. As you just heard, Jeanne Calment was dining on duck thighs and chocolate cake at the age of 120.

My opinion that most of us will slow down to a degree is based upon watching my parents, my in-laws, a few neighbors, and some colleagues. I have confirmed this phenomenon with friends we often see who graduated from high school 10 or so years ahead of me. Also, I have taken up this topic with financial planners. They have verified what I am seeing. Most, though not all, of their clients tend to stay closer to home as they enter and navigate their ninth decade on the planet. There is a smattering of common sense employed here, as well. Let's be honest. Human beings are not as sharp, energetic, or active as they age.

Now, this reality is nothing from which to shy away. Good planning requires honesty and being realistic.

Our spending will likely slow down with us. It is important to account for this fact in your planning. Hopefully, the mortgage is paid off and one is not tied up in a three-year lease on a sports coupe at age 77. If you agree with me so far, then can you also agree that our monetary needs are not going to grow steadily toward the heavens on a straight-line path?

If you can live comfortably on $100,000 per year at age 65, you are not likely going to require $263,881 annually at age 90 to meet your needs. Some simple retirement planning tools will suggest that your spending needs will more than double during the course of 25 years of retirement. Here's a straightforward example:

- Assume that you have assets to spend in your retirement of $2,685,695 at age 65
- Apply a 2% inflation rate
- Give yourself an annual yield of 6% on your dough

A planning tool will tell you that you will need to spend more than $263,000 at age 90 to have the equivalent of your $100,000 annual spend when you were 65.[2] This is scary. It is also, I think, not a realistic prediction

[2] Here are several lists of financial planning software that you may find helpful if you wish to plug in your numbers and see where you land: https://smartasset.com/financial-advisor/financial-planning-software; https://investorjunkie.com/retirement/best-free-retirement-planning-tools/; and https://www.dinkytown.net/java/retirement-planner-calculator.html.

of future spending. If you are like many people, one look at this scenario and the first question that pops into your head is, "How can I ever retire?"

Many online financial planning tools provoke thinking that I believe causes unnecessary anxiety. You have certainly heard that the successful formula for financial comfort in retirement is to have something on the

Exercise #1
Finding a Financial Planner

---

1. Identify three good friends whose opinions you respect.

2. Ask each of them if they have a financial advisor.

3. Ask if they are satisfied with the services they are being provided with and why.

4. Set up a time to chat with those advisors favorably recommended to you.

order of eight times your last working year's salary in the bank the day you quit working. I am sure you have been exposed to the suggestion that spending more than 4 percent of your savings each year in retirement could result in you running out of money. Now some advisors have scaled this back to 3.5 percent.

Take these assumptions and administer some simple math. You will find how unrealistic and perhaps unnecessary the notion that such large sums of money are required to successfully bow out and do what you want to do in life.

You may wish to personally enjoy a larger portion of the monetary fruits of your labor after working hard to create your new life or simply putting your working days behind you and retiring. This, too, is possible though it may require that you bend some financial planners' 4 percent withdrawal rule and do a little living.

THE GO YEARS, THE SLOW YEARS, AND THE GO-SLOW YEARS

Let me share with you two retirement planning scenarios—both are for a 39-year-old married lawyer with a working spouse. There are, of course, lots of other age groups, but this will help illustrate my point that you must create a financial plan personalized to your situation.

According to the Bureau of Labor Statistics in May 2021, the median salary for a lawyer in the United States was $127,990.[3] Our lawyer, Rene, is 39 years old, not a beginner and presumably well-established. I plugged her or him in my model with an income of $100,000 per year today.

Bear with me a second as I run through some numbers. You can be sure I enlisted expert help in putting this retirement scenario together. These are crucial to understanding how this works.

Here are the metrics and assumptions used when devising this couple's financial plan:

- Our lawyer, Rene, is age 39 with an annual income of $100,000.
- Rene's spouse, Jessie, is also age 39 with an annual income of $50,000.

---

[3] Bureau of Labor Statistics, U.S. Department of Labor. "Lawyers." *Occupational Outlook Handbook*, Updated September 8, 2022. https://www.bls.gov/ooh/legal/lawyers.htm.

- I had their incomes grow at the rate of 3 percent annually.
- They pay taxes and save for retirement. Their current annual after-tax spending is $80,000, which will increase at the rate of 2.5 percent to account for inflation. I get that this is an arbitrary number. It could be more. It could be less. Either way, inflation could impact their plan. But this is a model, so we're going with 2.5 percent today.[4]
- Our lawyer in 2021 has a 401K valued at $75,000, and our spouse has $25,000 in retirement savings.
- Rene and Jessie will both retire on Christmas Day 2048. I used this year to get them to their full retirement age as determined by the SSA. Part of their retirement will be funded by their return on the investment our couple made by contributing to social security all of their working days. They will wait to draw their social security checks until they reach age 70 in order to maximize their benefits.
- During the course of their remaining working lives—27 more years—they plan to put 10 percent of their annual incomes into retirement accounts, to be matched at the rate of 3 percent by their employers.
- The retirement accounts will grow at an average rate of 6 percent until they retire in 2048. Thereafter, they'll rebalance their portfolios a bit, and they will grow at an average rate of 5.5 percent per year going forward in retirement. Some years will be better; some will be terrible. Over the long haul, these rates of return are reasonable per my expert financial planners.
- I plugged in a 15 percent income tax rate and a 10 percent rate on capital gains in retirement.
- The plan takes them into their 90th year. Of course, we hope they live long and healthy lives that may go beyond 90 years. But I needed an end date to make sense of the data.

When Rene and Jessie have reached full retirement age—67 years old—their nest egg will have grown to $2,162,955. A nice sum to have in the bank to start their next chapter of life together. Now we need to look at

---

[4] Though in 2022 we experienced an annual inflation rate of 8 percent, according to *Forbes,* inflation averaged 1.88 percent during the past 10 years. See https://www.forbes.com/sites/qai/2023/01/02/is-inflation-high-compared-to-years-past-breaking-down-inflation-rates-by-year/.

their spending. It is their outlay that will dictate how well they are going to live. It will also tell us whether they will have to go back to work at age 75 because they ran out of money.

THE SIMPLE PLAN

First, let's look at what their path to financial success in retirement looks like using a simplistic planning tool, rote assumptions, and no accounting for their personal situation. It's a one-size-fits-all model using the standard planning tool numbers for what is needed in retirement.

Here are the variables for you:

- In the first year of their retirement, Rene and Jessie spend the equivalent of the $80,000 per year to live to which they were accustomed to when they were 39 years old.
- Their allowed spending I increased by 3 percent each year over their remaining 27 years at work.
- I've also added some discretionary expenses. There's an extra $5,000 annually for 15 years for travel, $6,000 for healthcare, and $20,000 each to replace their automobiles every 10 years.
- These spending rates will continue to grow at 2.5 percent per year during their retirement.

They are going to live well unless they go off the rails and spend wildly.

If they spend precisely what they are allowed and otherwise stick to this model, in their first full year of retirement, they will have $194,680 to spend. Amazing when you use the impact of inflation to predict our monetary needs long into the future.

If their portfolios continue to increase at the rate of 5.5 percent after retirement, and all our other variables remain the same, there should still be money in the pot when they reach 90. In fact, it looks like a lot, $963,000. But there is a huge risk with this model, which I'll discuss in a minute.

THE PERSONALIZED PLAN

Now let's put further thought into our couple's plan. I am going to employ the savings and personal spending strategy that Patty and I put in place with our advisor. Let's tweak the standard retirement planning program and see if Rene and Jessie land more securely in retirement. I'll illustrate the difference and the flexibility you create for yourself by taking the time to develop a personal plan. There is nothing particularly sophisticated about it. It's a function of understanding your finances, being realistic in your spending goals, and having the right financial advisor to steer you on course.

We asked our advisor to work with us in developing a realistic spending plan. We worked together to experiment with our numbers. Over a period of about 10 years, we played with this a lot. Patty and I tweaked it. We changed the estimated returns, modified the inflation factor, and threw in hypothetical, dream—read expensive—vacations.

I pestered our advisor with ideas and questions. At some point, I was regularly apologizing to him for coming up with another concept as we talked. Sometimes I'd return home from our meeting and email him an idea I had in the car upon leaving his office. I wanted to know the impact of our plan on every little twist that came to mind. I was determined to gain the confidence that once I pulled the trigger, I would have no risk of returning to the workforce, standing at the end of the checkout line wearing a brightly colored vest.

If I wished to pack away my suits and ties at age 65, we envisioned that in the following 8 years, from age 65 to 73, we'd be active. We could travel to places we'd not seen. Maybe take our kids and grandchildren on trips. The first eight years of retirement would be more expensive than the last eight.

So, we devised our plan accordingly for the Go-Go Years.

I've no plan that when I turn 73 years old to stop and take up a front porch swing and watch the world go by. However, it's not unrealistic to believe that at some point in the second 8 years of retirement, ages 73 to 81, will begin to be less expensive than the first 8 years. Maybe we will take fewer trips, drink cheaper wine, and no longer maintain the family home with a pool and amenities of a family of five. We again tweaked the spending part of our plan to see what happened if we planned to spend less money in those second 8 years of no paychecks leading to my 81st birthday. These are the Go-Slow Years.

I've not met anyone who, at age 65, was looking forward to being 81 years old. I'm not either, but it beats the alternative. There's nothing I can do to make the clock run backward. If I'm lucky, one day, I'll be 81. If you want a proper plan, you need to take a moment and think about what life in your eighth decade may look like. We're all different. Perhaps 36 rounds of golf, 40-mile bike rides, and a dinner out 3 times a week are in the cards for some octogenarians. Others, not so much. In our plan, we trimmed back our spending at the point of me entering the world of my ninth decade in contemplation of the likely reality. We'll likely be moving about less and moving slower when we are moving. These may be the "go-slow years."

I prepared the chart below to illustrate how personalizing our couple's spending over the course of retirement looks compared to the straight-line approach. Beginning at age 73, the customized plan—the dashed line—envisions spending less per year. A similar downward adjustment is made at age 81.

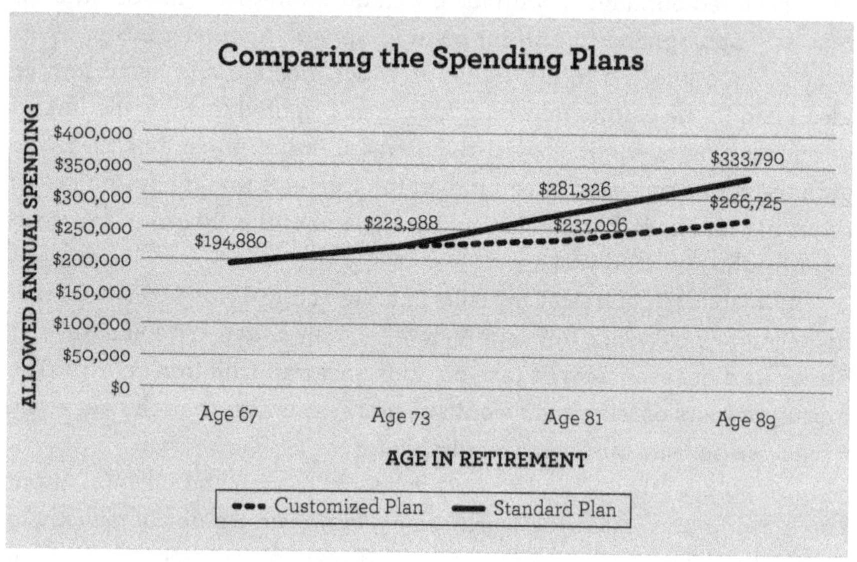

Source: Michael Wright.

The standard planning tool—the solid line—is telling Jessie and Rene that their spending pattern won't change from age 67 to when they're 89 years old. It's going to keep shooting upward. That's not likely to be the case in my view. Relying on a financial plan that is not personalized can lead to frustration. The nest egg needed to retire gracefully—and securely—may appear out of reach.

By slowly decreasing the spending during the second eight years, then reducing it for the third 8-year period of their retirement, our couple should have nearly twice as much left at age 90 than with the standard model: $2,000,000 versus $963,000. It's a big difference. What does it mean?

MONTE CARLO SIMULATION

Before getting to the answer, I want to tell you about a tool that will test your plan and provide you with confidence that you are on a glide path to retirement or career-change success. Generally speaking, these financial planning models are tested using what is called the Monte Carlo Simulation.

We've all seen James Bond, trim and smart in his tuxedo, a martini waiting as he rolls dice in the swank casino in Monaco. Though James wins more often than others at the table, he is still engaging in games of chance wherein the outcome is unpredictable. Your retirement planning has unknown variables, the same as Bond's craps table in Monte Carlo.

Having your financial plan created with the help of a professional will likely entail it being tested using a Monte Carlo Simulation. The operator of my computer—me—doesn't have the requisite knowledge to try doing this at home.

The Monte Carlo Simulation takes its name from that idyllic city on the Mediterranean where Agent 007 and others with a passion for gambling, the wardrobe, and resources do it in style. It is a statistical simulation of the unpredictable variables that go into financial planning. The model evaluates different outcomes in a process—here, financial planning—that cannot be accurately predicted due to influences that are variable. Nobody knows when they are going to leave the planet, a key date for an entirely accurate financial plan. The market is not predictable, so the growth rate of your portfolio is an educated guess. Inflation and taxation are among other variables that cannot be nailed down in order to generate a 100 percent accurate prediction of what resources you will need 30 years after you are off the payroll.

Using the simulation, your plan will be tested for its viability with all the variables considered. All conceivable upsides, downsides, and uncertain factors are run through the computer multiple times, thousands of times. Using this planning tool enhances the ability to determine the likelihood that your plan will succeed. You don't want to be polishing your résumé in your dotage instead of taking a cruise.

I'm simplifying this a bit as I'm not a financial planner, but I want to share what I learned along the way to provide you with questions for the professionals you bring on board. I want you to get safely to the point where you can make a change in your life without waking up at two o'clock in the morning worrying about running out of money.

OUR COUPLE'S LIKELIHOOD OF SUCCESS

Having more than $900,000 on hand at age 90 seems adequate. In fact, it sounds darn good. If our couple reaches a point where they no longer have use for it, there could be some smiling heirs or grateful charities to enjoy the money. After spending at a good, but not lavish, clip through a long retirement, there's going on $1 million still in the accounts. The funds along with their social security checks will last until . . . well, you know. The other planning model, where we reduced Jessie and Rene's spending over the years, leaves them with more than $2 million. What's the point of dying with all that money in the bank?

Here's the catch. You have to take into account that a financial plan produces results based on the information put into it. It is then shaken and stirred using a Monte Carlo Simulation, which produces a model. This model is not a guarantee. There is only going to be $900,000 left at age 90 if the computer simulation accurately predicted the impact of every variable it used when it was run. What are the odds of that? In the course of creating a spending plan, these financial planning tools also provide the rate of the likelihood of success.

Here's the kicker for our couple if they rely upon straight-line spending. They have about a 50 percent chance of success. Yep, there is a 50/50 chance of failure, which means cutting back on spending to avoid the doomsday event—running out of money. It's not a bet I would be willing to take. I'd look for better odds before slowing down and accepting a pay cut. Looking at the projected $900,000 at age 90 and adopting that retirement plan might fail. Then what?

By taking the exact same resources and applying a personalized spending plan, the odds of success for Rene and Jesse increase to around 80 percent. Now we're talking. Unless you are a real risk-taker, this is more in the ballpark of reasonableness for retirement planning.

Patty and I were not satisfied at 80 percent when doing our planning. Creating a model that increases the likelihood of success can be done by manipulating the data you put into the program. You can get as close as possible to 100 percent by reducing the desired spending, adding more savings, or changing the rate of return on investments. This is where continually tinkering with your plan with the help of a knowledgeable advisor pays off.

ONCE YOU HAVE A PLAN, THEN WHAT?

Keep informed and approach your advisor with ideas about managing your plan and the investment vehicles selected. Be proactive in creating your plan. Ask lots of questions and challenge the results from time to time. We discovered that the further along we rode toward my transition to another way of spending my weekdays, the more we paid attention to what we were spending.

Test this on your financial advisor. A straight-line analysis—where your resources are plugged in, your life expectancy estimated, and an inflation factor assigned—will not generate the kind of report you may want to rely upon. It's a good starting point, but you don't want to quit your day job based on the information this planning tool provides. You need to drill down on your numbers and then feed them into a program designed to personalize what you have and how much you are going to spend during the course of your nonworking years.

The closer I got to bidding adieu to a paycheck, the more often we began to ask our advisor to test our plan. We would adjust the anticipated rate of return, test the impact of an increase or a decrease in planned spending, and play with the rate of inflation our models assumed. There are variables, some of which we can't control. When the day came to pull the trigger and walk away, we wanted to be certain that we'd run through as many possible scenarios as we could conjure up. We wanted to eliminate any nagging worries that we'd outlive our resources. We created a great partnership wherein our advisor brought to the table the knowledge, experience, and resources to help guide us to the financial place we believed we wanted to be.

Look at the difference in where Rene and Jessie end up depending on which spending model they rely upon. You can appreciate why Patty and I chose the personalized approach to plotting our future spending. We scaled it to our projected lifestyle. It's also easy to see why I was so immensely discouraged when I reviewed the results produced by retirement calculators run earlier in my process of thinking about hanging it up. I'd never be able to accumulate the resources these numbers told us we'd need to allow me to slow down, switch professions, or retire. The computations that envisioned that our spending would continue to increase at a static rate until death was depressing. For most of us, it's also inaccurate.

We are not going to keep doing those things that will keep us spending money at the rate we did at age 39.

I can't tell you what your number—how much you need in the bank to change the course of your life—will be. I assure you that number will change over the years if you continue to give thought to your financial future. Work toward that with your financial advisor and accountant. Michael Wright, our financial advisor, shared with me that "the assessment tools now available to sophisticated advisors go beyond measuring the level of our clients' risk tolerance when investing. They have evolved into acquiring data to understand the client's needs, not just how much money they have."

Exercise #2

Questions FOR Your Financial Adviser

1. Do I really need $3 million to retire and live a decent life?

2. How do I tweak the numbers?

Exercise #3

Questions FROM Your Financial Adviser

Be prepared to answer questions from your financial adviser by preparing for the following in advance:

1. What are my short-term financial needs?

2. Do I need to provide financially over the long term for my kids, parents, or favorite uncle?

3. Is it important that I bestow upon family, friends, or that favorite nephew an inheritance?

4. How much do I want to leave to my favorite charity, church, or university?

IT IS NEVER TOO LATE TO START

Until I was in my early 50s and became serious about making a change in my life, I was fearful that I would never be able to retire. As we wrote tuition checks, paid fees for sports clubs, took some nice trips, and kept the mortgage current, any talk of slowing down was muffled by the reality of living paycheck to paycheck. One look at an online financial planning tool would send me into a funk. I'd see that my future on this lawyering treadmill would never stop.

Relying on simple straight-line planning tools can scare people into the corner of an "I can never retire/slow down/do something else" mindset. I say this because it was our experience, too. It is this trap of despair that I want you to avoid.

It took a few years to develop the plan that allowed me to stop filling out my timesheet every day. It is not something we worked on every day—or even every month. In the early days, we met our financial advisor once a year. We increased that to twice a year, then around four times yearly as we were developing this plan. Now we meet with Michael a couple of times a year with some phone meetings in between to plan for our cash needs and review our spending strategy. Seek out a qualified financial advisor that meets your needs and get started.

You will need to revisit the topic of finances. There is no one-size-fits-all financial plan. Creating your plan will take time. It will evolve during the years as you grow closer to the day you wish to hang it up. Don't be discouraged if you think you are off to a slow start or that you came late to this part of the future-planning game. It is never too late to get started on a financial plan.

11

You Gotta Have a Plan

> "There are two kinds of forecasters: those who don't know, and those who don't know they don't know."[1]
>
> —John Kenneth Galbraith, Canadian-American economist (1908–2006)

So, what do you want to be when you grow up? No matter where you are in your career, you should ask yourself this question every so often—no need to restrict yourself. If you wish, think big and start moving in another direction with purpose. On the other hand, perhaps you're generally content but interested in a tweak or two in your professional or personal life. Nothing will happen without some investment of your time, among other things. But it's making the first move—by putting your valuable time into the project—that will get it started.

A few decades back, I picked up our son at daycare. It happened to be the day that the four-year-old children were asked about their future career plans. There was a poster that ran the height of the door on which it was announced to the world that Sean McGoff wanted to be Batman when he grew up. We thought it was great. Among the fireman, baseball players, and Internet tycoons from his generation, our son would be Batman.

For reasons long forgotten, Sean had second thoughts a few days later. He reported to his teacher that he was abandoning his goal of becoming the Caped Crusader. He switched his intended career path from a billionaire superhero in favor of something less exciting, but more in line with

[1] Galbraith, John Kenneth. "Quotefancy." 1993. https://quotefancy.com/quote/1199214/John-Kenneth-Galbraith-There-are-two-kinds-of-forecasters-those-who-don-t-know-and-those.

the dreams of the other four-year-olds sitting on the floor around the room. An apparent attack of peer pressure struck Sean at four years of age. We were robbed of having a superhero in the family. It was our son's first step in career planning.

After deciding to forgo a career as Batman, Sean taught fifth grade and coached soccer before going to law school. He was a financial advisor for a short time. He worked his way along and is presently the chief compliance officer in the legal department of an insurance company. We still have his Batman cape. Should Sean decide to return to the earlier fork in the road to chase his then-dream job, we're prepared to help with his wardrobe.

HELP IS ON THE WAY

We spend our entire careers asking questions. Trial lawyers attend training programs to learn how to ask good questions. We query our clients, experts, and opposing counsel all day long. When we get home in the evening, we round out our day by cross-examining the family at the dinner table. Lawyers know how to ask good questions.

This skill needs to go to work for us as we plan our futures. There is much to be learned from others who developed talents and expertise different than our own. A jumping-off point is to identify where you could use assistance by honestly evaluating your needs, strengths, and the gaps to be filled by experts.

I had three professional advisors whom I could depend upon to guide me in areas where I needed expert advice: our accountant, our financial advisor, and the career coach I hired in 2007. Three people, that's a small team. It was all the professional support we felt we needed to help us in achieving our goals.

I had lots of informal advisors that have answered my questions and guided me along from boyhood. It would not be fair or accurate to say our three professional advisors were the only contributors to the plan. My parents and siblings certainly helped. Much was learned at Dad's knee starting when I was young. My brother Terry and I would stand next to our father while he shaved in the morning, peppering him with questions. He never chased us away. Though some of his answers were tongue-in-cheek, Dad was happy to give us his two cents' worth on whatever topic we brought up. As we became teenagers, he was even more generous with his thoughts, offering regular, unsolicited "recommendations" to his six children.

Chatting with my adult brothers and sisters, we compared notes about what we were doing in our lives. This is one of the many advantages of being a part of a big family. I've garnered a number of unvarnished opinions from the younger brothers I used to rough up in the yard when Mom was distracted with another of the six kids. Siblings have a way of letting you know when you are getting farfetched with your ideas.

Don't rule out business partners, good friends, and others who have trodden this path before you. I'm not suggesting you lay out your finances over a cup of coffee with your sorority sister, army buddy, or college roommate, but comparing notes with someone you trust and with whom you are comfortable will provide you with insight. The more information you gather, the better the decisions you will arrive at.

Executive coach for lawyers Anna Rappaport says, "As you muster the courage to make a change, you need to have a support system. There are organizations dedicated to almost any path you are pursuing. There you can find not only information and resources, but also new friends whom you can call upon for advice at key junctures."[2] She suggests that one have a community of support, not just one person. It pays to look beyond the easy asks such as a significant other, a fishing buddy, or a sorority sister. If your plan is to trade in the stress of being a litigator for what you believe will be a life of ease as an estate planner, then join the Trusts and Estates section of the bar. Your eyes may be opened as to how that segment of the bar operates. You'll also meet your next group of colleagues, some of whom may help with your transformation.

Borrowing from JK Galbraith's blunt assessment of experts in his discipline, let's start by identifying what areas of future planning you may not know or do not feel you grasp well. Next, give some thought to whom you might know who will help you out or steer you in the right direction.

---

[2] From my personal conversation with Anna Rappaport.

Exercise #1
Your Most Important Resources

List the three most important resources you might access to help you reach your goals:

1.

2.

3.

PUT THE PENCIL TO IT

"Kev, you need to put the pencil to it." This was one of my father's pet phrases and you've seen it a couple of times already. I can't tell you how many times I heard this tip being offered in our house when I was growing up. He had other words of wisdom that still roll around in my head. I passed this one, and other nuggets on to our children from time to time. They rolled their eyes the same as I did when I heard these tidbits from my dad as a kid.

Growing up, Dad kept a keen eye on our homework. He was the manager of planning and forecasting at Bryant Manufacturing. He plotted the number of furnaces and air conditioners the factory should make each year.

As we sat at the dining room table after dinner doing our assignments, he combed over the notes and spreadsheets he had brought home from work. It was rare that a school assignment or a difficult question any of us posed to Dad wasn't met with him clearing his throat before answering with: "You need to put the pencil to it."

Patty had worked at the beauty shop for two years when the owner decided to move to Colorado. She offered to sell the business to Patty, who was 22 years old. I was a first-year law student making $15 a game refereeing football a couple of afternoons a week. Patty was doing well but just getting established in her profession. We were frugal out of necessity. There was not much to spend. We lived paycheck to paycheck.

The boss wanted $40,000 for her shop, which included everything. It was a well-established business. The location was great, and there were hairdressers working for the shop on commission occupying most of the chairs.

When my father heard of the opportunity, he suggested that we ask for the company's books. After culling through five years of tax returns and combing over the other financial records provided, Dad put the pencil to it. He drafted a business plan. On paper, it looked viable. Then there was the issue of money. We had none.

We took Pop's pro forma to the bank branch located next to the shop. We both knew the manager. He was four years older than me. He had attended the same grade school and high school as I had. His mom picked me up on her way to work at Brebeuf Preparatory School, giving me a ride to school in my freshman and sophomore years of high school.

Our prospective banker reviewed the work Dad had put the pencil to. He was satisfied that we could repay the loan. He did ask for insurance in the form of the signatures of both of our parents, people he'd known since he was a kid. The bank loaned us $20,000, and the owner financed the other $20,000, which we paid down monthly. We shared a nice bottle of Chateau Margaux with our parents the day the bank loan was satisfied, and they were off the hook. The empty bottle stands as a trophy in our kitchen.

PLANNING AT WORK, NOT AT HOME

A lawyer's commitment to the office is a devotion unlike any other, but this loyalty is not unique to the law business. My sense is that there is a point in a lawyer's career where most of the energy for creativity and strategic thinking is employed at work. Doing our clients' bidding can leave little stamina—or time—for reflecting on ourselves.

One day, I was chatting with my mom about our annual trip to Cleveland to visit family. She waxed on, using her occasional sarcastic tone for emphasis: "That father of yours, he never left home without that damn briefcase."

Our family station wagon would be stuffed with six kids. One of us was up front with Mom and Dad. The rest staked our real estate in the back of the car, which we shared with a picnic lunch, assorted books and games, and the briefcase. The baggage rode on top. Strapped to a rickety luggage carrier, the suitcases, repurposed plastic bags from the dry cleaners, and a gym bag carrying all of our belongings were covered by a well-worn tarp. It kept most of the rain off our things during the six-to-eight-hour drive to our one-week vacation.

When the opportunity was presented, I, too, was guilty of never leaving on vacation without "that damn briefcase." I learned from the best. I also inherited a smidgen of the planning gene from my dad. Though I didn't always employ it effectively, it was useful when it came time to build a law firm.

SMALL TASKS WILL CREATE BIG ACCOMPLISHMENTS

I represented a man in a triple homicide prosecution. The litigation went on for more than seven years. I tried the case three times. It was the most interesting, exhilarating, frustrating, and satisfying case I had in my 40 years in practice.

At the outset, the State identified 200 witnesses. We received thousands of pages in discovery, including police reports, witness statements, and the work of experts from the FBI and other agencies. Some of the documents turned over to us were not organized, tendered in the order in which they fell out of the copier. It was a daunting project. Where to start?

Along with my co-counsel, paralegal, law clerks, and investigator, we dug in. Preparing our defense became more complicated. The more work we did, the more there was to do. Instead of whittling down the to-do lists, the tasks ahead ballooned. Organizing the files so they were accessible, chasing leads, and devising a defense strategy made more work for us.

The first trial took place 12 years after the crimes. This meant our investigator had to run down witnesses long after the events. Some had moved. The memories of others had faded. We never located some folks we'd have liked to have interviewed. We were adding more things to our to-do list than we were ticking off as completed.

There were times when I was overwhelmed, but I had a great team working with me. We managed to plow through our endless to-do lists and sub-lists. Little by little, we whittled away at our checklists. The judge's gavel struck the bench calling the case three years after the charges were filed. We were organized and prepared for trial.

At the time I undertook my client's defense, I had been in practice for around 19 years. I knew my best approach to tackling big projects. The work had to be broken down into bits and pieces. Otherwise, I would spin my wheels and grab at random tasks. There would be no order to things. I would never be properly organized. Nothing would be done well.

Baby steps. Breaking off a bit at a time. Making a big project a series of small projects. There are many ways to characterize this approach to a plan. It's worked for me as a lawyer. You will increase the likelihood of success with your personal plan if you employ a method that energizes you.

What seems easy will become tedious if the path to the endgame looks too steep. The step-by-step approach works. I'm willing to bet you have employed it in your practice, the same as I did over the years.

Employ this skill that you developed as a lawyer. Put the incremental approach to attaining goals outside the office to work as you plan your future. Like my trial prep, what we do every day has application outside the law business. Ticking off the "accomplished" box on your to-do list doesn't always have to be associated with the office.

You'll achieve a measure of satisfaction by seeing each day as part of your strategy. You don't need to carve out hours for this endeavor. The thinking and planning can be relegated to 15 or 30 minutes at a time. Eating lunch at your desk again? Turn off your emails, shut down the beeps and buzzing notifications your phone is producing, and squeeze out a few moments to think about yourself.

IDENTIFY WHAT YOU WANT

Without goals, no plan will work. It's important to take the time to reflect. January 1st is the traditional day for jotting down resolutions to fail at during the upcoming months. Any day is a good day to start setting goals. You can't have a plan without a goal. Without a goal, it's easy to fall into a rut, stalled by the side of the road. You cannot have a goal without taking the time to think about what it is you're looking for—what do you want? I spoke with executive coach for lawyers Anna Rappaport about goal setting. She shared with me the following about the importance of integrating values into the process of planning a major life change:

> When contemplating a significant life change, it is critically important to clarify your values. What values are most important for you personally to have a satisfying and rewarding life? How important is money, status, learning and growth, love and connection, making a difference, etc.? Clarifying your values serves two important purposes. First, it helps you to set goals and make decisions that will lead to the greatest satisfaction. Second, it helps you make the leap between wanting something and actually doing it. It takes a lot of courage to make any kind of big change. But a change that involves giving up significant money and status and leaving behind wonderful work colleagues is extraordinarily challenging. The more clarity you have that this change is really aligned with your values and your purpose, the more easily you will be able to overcome this hurdle and pursue your passions.

Arm yourself with a handpicked team of advisors. Your lineup may include 2 people or 10. Bring on mentors, accountants, coaches, and professionals with the skills and expertise that you are seeking. Friends, professional colleagues, and family should be sought out to join. Not every advisor has to be paid to qualify as a part of your posse. Some of the best advice you'll ever receive may be over a beer with a trusted friend. That said, do not be a cheapskate. Hire and pay the professionals you need on your team, and don't begrudge their fees. Getting solid professional advice to help get you to where you want to be will be some of the best money you have ever spent.

Exercise #2

Create Your Action Plan

Create an action plan to begin accomplishing that one objective you can start on now.

1. Identify the objective.

2. Write out what you will need to do to get there.

3. Now, break it down into manageable pieces; create a path to regular accomplishments.

4. Calendar time each week to either reflect on your goal or to work on it.

5. Hold yourself accountable by:
   - Telling someone that you're working on this goal. Choose someone who will be honest with you in your discussions about your goal and will follow up and ask how your work is coming along.
   - Put on your calendar the dates by which you will accomplish each of the steps required to achieve your goal.
   - Today is a great day to get started. Put the pencil to it.

JANE RUEMMELE: MOM, WIFE, LAWYER, GAME MAKER

In 1994, 10 years after graduating from law school, Jane Ruemmele was making her way as a criminal defense lawyer in Indianapolis. She was trying cases as a public defender. At the same time, she was investigating and preparing matters next in line for trial or resolution. At home, she and her husband Stephen were occupied with two young boys separated in age by only 18 months.

Although busy with her practice, Jane made time for other passions. She carved out time to read, especially about history. Jane came to appreciate that history is about how the world changed and not simply an endless progression of dates marking battles and shifting of borders, or a list of leaders come and gone.

Jane honed her creative talents while providing entertainment for her two little boys. "I come from a family of game players," Jane told me. "My dad taught me how to play chess, and I passed this on to our children." Her interest in history mingled with her love of games brought about an idea that directed Jane toward a unique business venture: She became a game maker.

Taking a packet of index cards, Jane wrote a historical event on each one. She then challenged her sons to organize them in chronological sequence. "A good game makes you think," per Jane. Her boys liked the challenge presented by the game their mom invented for them. She took her stack of index cards to the boys' grade school. Jane and their teachers watched a class of eight- and nine-year-olds play the first iteration of what would become Jane's game Chronology.[3]

To develop Chronology into a marketable product, Jane took a brief break from her law office. She accompanied her husband on a business trip to Seattle. While Stephen worked, Jane spent the week in a coffee shop with a stack of books. In 1994, a Google search was a thing of the future. There was no technology available to instantaneously provide the data for her game using a search query. Jane's source material came from the shelves of the public library. She scoured the *New York Times* Timeline of Events for

[3] Buffalo Games & Puzzles. "Chronology." Accessed April 26, 2023. https://buffalogames.com/chronology/.

historically important facts to include on her cards. The questions for Jane's game were written down, then every fact was verified by two independent sources.

Six months after her work at the coffee shop, Jane identified a publisher. Her game was being sold in stores by 1996. Chronology became a bestselling game in Sweden. Today it's sold in the U.S. and is still popular in Sweden, as well as in Poland and Norway. You'll find the 20th-anniversary edition of Chronology on Amazon.

Jane merged her interests, talents, and background in law to become a game maker. She didn't quit her day job practicing law, which she still thoroughly enjoys. Developing Chronology was a family affair. Her initial stack of index cards was developed to keep her boys busy. Husband Stephen designed the first edition of Chronology.

Jane sold the rights to the game she invented. The royalty checks are deposited into her bank account every three months. Chronology provides another income stream for Jane and her family. She made certain that all her eggs were not in one basket, a lesson her father taught her when she was a young girl.

Jane commented to me that "each of our clients represents a project. For me, developing Chronology was another project. We should give our own projects the same attention that we give to our clients' projects."

Perhaps you have a passion or a talent set aside in favor of your law work. Consider devoting some time like Jane did to get one of your personal projects off the ground. You don't have to quit your day job to find a meaningful side gig that invigorates you. It may even provide you with another paycheck.

PART IV

From Plan to Reality

I feel free. This phrase resonates when not just read. It works best for me when I hear the words "I feel free" put into song. I recommend you experience it. Take a break and listen to *I Feel Free* by the rock group Cream.[1] The refrain is one earworm you won't want to chase away when your plan comes together.

Once the hard work is done and your vision is in place, you can sit back and relax, right? Not exactly. I was talking to a friend from high school. He saw a doctor because he thought he may have had a stroke. The doc told him, "That wasn't a stroke; it was a fainting spell. My advice to you is to keep moving." The patient continues his work as an entrepreneur into his 70th year. He's not stopping. You must do the same if you are to succeed.

Your plan is a means to an end. It is not "The End." It is another beginning. If your choice is to cut back and do other things, you are going to be busy. If you retire and take up a hobby or start a new gig, time will still be a precious commodity, just like it was when you were billing your clients. What you may find is the pace is more leisurely and the deadlines a bit squishy.

When a call comes across for an impromptu round of golf or lunch with a friend, it's easier to say yes.

---

1 Cream. "I Feel Free." *Fresh Cream*. New York: Atco, 1966.

In the old days, it was required to say no because “I have a brief due or a deal closing.” We were too busy.

You still must get things done. The difference is now you are the keeper of the schedule. You list the priorities and get to postpone things that can be put off in favor of what you want to do. Being the master of your time doesn’t mean you’ll sit and do nothing. You will just operate at a pace most convenient to you. This will be a huge and welcome change in how you manage your time. The song will buzz in your head. You’ll feel free.

12

Circling Back: Some Goals Need to Germinate

> "The greatest danger for most of us is not that our aim is too high and we miss it, but that it is too low and we reach it."[1]
>
> —Michelangelo, Italian artist and scientist (1475–1564)

I spent 15 months in Europe when I was 18 years old, stationed by the U.S.Army in Germany. I later had an opportunity to return to Europe to study international business through the McGeorge School of Law Master of Laws (LLM) program. As I told you earlier, I was accepted into the program at the same time that I received a job offer with the law firm in Greenfield, Indiana. For some, this would be an easy decision either way—but for Patty and me, the best way to proceed was far from clear. Here's the rest of that story.

During the first seven years of our marriage, Patty and I had vacationed in Germany and France three times. Except for a three-week journey when I finished college, the trips were never for more than two weeks. Our European experience together was a grand total of 7 weeks out of the 84 months we had been married. We weren't proficient in any language other than English and had no money.

On the other hand, we owned a small house and were purchasing Patty's salon, putting us around $100,000 in manageable debt. "Manageable," that is if we were both receiving a paycheck. Were our thoughts of living in France nothing more than the wishful thinking that many voyagers, young and old, engage in when exposed to foreign lands?

Sheldon Breskow, my boss at the disciplinary commission, convinced me that France would always be there. The country wasn't going anywhere.

---

1 BrainyQuote. "Michelangelo Quotes." Accessed April 26, 2023. https://www.brainyquote.com/quotes/michelangelo_108779.

Visit often, if you wish and are able to do so, he suggested. There will be time one day for long stays in France if that's something you want to do. He was direct, leaning forward with his finger wagging, *telling* me that for now you need to take the path most compatible with your skills and your present situation. The message Sheldon delivered was straightforward. "Now that we've analyzed the facts, the proper course is obvious."

I chose Greenfield, Indiana, over Paris, France. It's easy to get a chuckle out of people when I tell them, without burdening them with the facts, that I turned down a position in Paris, France, in favor of a job in Greenfield, Indiana. It was the right direction, the proper fork in the road for us to take. Sheldon was right. France was always there.

Patty and I traveled to France for a few weeks almost every summer of our marriage. We long ago lost count of how many times we have visited France over the years since I followed Sheldon's advice and made the decision to hone my Indiana lawyering skills. We've traveled all over the French countryside. We made friends in Europe along the way, some of whom we correspond with and visit from time to time. We took our kids along on several vacations. We studied the language to become proficient. We now live part of the year in the south of France. The opportunity to do so presented itself only because I was voted off the management committee—the best election I ever lost.

HAPPENING UPON PROVENCE

It was again a stroke of serendipity that steered our ship. The Languedoc is the region of France that runs along the Mediterranean to the Pyrenees on the Spanish border. It is populated with coastal villages and mountain hamlets. Beginning in 2008, Patty and I had enjoyed four or five pleasant trips to the region, always renting an ancient stone home in a small village. We met the mayor, befriended the couple whose home we rented, and casually looked at some properties with the idea of a second home in the area. But we thought it foolish to have a vacation home 5,000 miles from where we lived. We talked ourselves out of it and didn't act on our idea of buying property in France.

Once more, events beyond our control intervened, sending us—literally—in a different direction. It altered our path. When I arranged to again reserve the house we had previously rented, the owner told me that if his mother-in-law came from Germany for a visit, we would have to find other accommodations. She had first dibs on the apartment. As luck would have it, his mother-in-law scheduled her visit during our planned week. Patty and I decided to venture to another region of France during our trip in the early fall of 2011.

We settled upon Provence, a part of France we had not deeply explored in our travels. After losing our rental in favor of our host's family member, we booked an apartment in L'Isle sur la Sorgue. We'd been there on a day trip 15 years earlier. The town is known for its antique dealers and a lively Sunday market. We enjoyed a fall week in Provence, taking day trips from our base in the center of the ancient town. The people were friendly, the weather heavenly, and the region afforded many things to do. We thought maybe we'd be back one day. Then we returned to our daily lives in Indiana, working and raising our children.

HOW I WON THE LOST ELECTION

You'll recall how I wasn't re-elected to the firm's management committee and mentioned that this was the best election I'd ever lost. Until I got voted off the management committee, I don't know that I had ever lost an election. I was president of the student council in high school, president of the student bar association in law school, and served as president of the Indianapolis Bar Association. I was board chair for The Cabaret, an arts organization in Indianapolis, for three years and held the same role for the public defender's council back in the day. It was a bit of a sting to be the runner-up in a two-person race.

Living the life of a busy professional, you appreciate the feeling when a block of time suddenly opens on your calendar. Most times, it is liberating. Many cases settle on the courthouse steps. If I was in "trial prep mode," lots of things were pushed aside in the days—or weeks for bigger cases—prior to the first day of trial. The calendar was blocked off for however long it was estimated a case might take to try. Settling a matter to my client's satisfaction had an added benefit. My schedule had a big and welcomed gap in it where I'd blocked out the time for the trial that would now not happen. I almost always appreciated the opportunity to catch up or take some time to recover from the stress of pulling everything together for a trial.

Given my second-place finish in the firm election, I struck from my calendar the numerous firm management meetings and attendant obligations. Those duties now belonged to the victor. Most of January 2012 now sat open on my calendar. Patty and I decided not to waste this unplanned freedom. The first months of the year in Indiana are gray, cold, and a bit dreary. We had never been to France in January, and we knew that the sun shines in the south of France in wintertime. We booked the same apartment we'd rented in the fall and in January 2012 returned to L'Isle sur la Sorgue to pass 10 days.

Among the many restaurants, shops, and hair salons in the town, there are a plethora of real estate agencies. As there is no multiple listing system in France, agents promote their stock of properties with photos in shop windows and catalogs for the taking from a metal box by the agency's door. We spent the time looking at the properties for sale by the various *agences immobilières,* casually looking without being serious about purchasing an apartment in France.

In the course of booking our rental, we had struck up a conversation with the owners. Judy and Harry live part of the year in California. They were at the time spending five months or so out of the year in their French *pied a terre,* renting it to others when they returned to California. In a phone call they kindly explained to us in detail the economics of owning a rental property in Provence. L'Isle sur la Sorgue is a popular tourist destination and, unlike some of the smaller villages in the area, is vibrant year-round. The rental market was good. On a small property, a modest number of weeks rented would generate sufficient income to pay the cost of managing the property, plus the taxes, insurance, and utilities.

During several conversations with our new, long-distance friends, Patty and I were tutored on how to manage a property 5,000 miles from our home. Harry and Judy promised to connect us with the person caring for their apartment as a possible resource to manage ours. They had a line on a banker and an insurance agent. Our interest was piqued. I was working a lot, but we thought that if we owned a place, we could still visit two or three times a year.

We spent the next few days looking more intently at the adverts in the agency windows. We popped into several and told the agents what we were looking for: a small apartment in the city center with a terrace or some other outdoor space. At every turn, we were told that this was a tall order. *"Impossible, monsieur,"* we heard multiple times. Finding an apartment in the middle of town meeting our requirement for outdoor space would be difficult. They are few and far between in the center of the ancient town. After looking at a few unacceptable options, we were mildly disappointed. This wasn't something we needed to do. It sounded fun. We'd always wanted to live in France, and this seemed like the opportunity to find a property we could afford, as we would have no expenses if rented as planned.

In the evenings, we sat on the terrace of Judy and Harry's apartment. They had a nice outdoor space. There were plants and herbs growing in pots next to the table. We were shaded by a large round umbrella that sat beneath the small terrace of the apartment above. We commiserated over a glass of local wine, lamenting that it was unlikely we'd find an apartment in the village. There was nothing about which to be too disappointed if this venture didn't pan out. We didn't come to Provence house hunting. We were hiding for a few weeks avoiding part of another Midwestern winter.

One morning, I was returning to the apartment with a warm baguette tucked under my arm when I saw a sign—a literal sign—that would put our plan in motion. We had a little more than one week left of our trip. The apartment-buying idea was fading. As I entered the small square where we were staying, I looked up at our bedroom window overlooking the shops. Tacked to the shutter of the apartment above our rental, the one with a terrace, was a sign, *"A Vendre"*—For Sale. We'd been there for a week and had never noticed the for-sale sign. There did exist an apartment for sale with outdoor space in the center of the town. I dialed the realtor immediately.

Jean Christophe was gracious and accommodating. He showed us the apartment four times in five days. The place was small, 33 square meters or 355 square feet. The terrace overlooked the rooftops of L'Isle sur la Sorgue from the second floor of the building. To make it suitable, we would need to move two walls and cut a hole in another. It needed work, and our trip was coming to an end.

Harry and Judy connected us to their friend, who had remodeled their apartment and managed their rentals. Luckily, her boyfriend was in the construction business. He came over and inspected the heating and electrical systems, as well as the structure, and gave us a thumbs up. Now, Patty and I were in a real quandary: should we buy or not?

We had found an apartment we wanted in a locale we liked. The price was right. Harry and Judy had introduced us to the team we would need to make the purchase, remodel the property, and manage our rentals. But did this make any sense? We went back and forth up to the day we had to leave

France. We drove to Marseille early in the morning to begin the journey home. Patty and I discussed the apartment throughout the hour-long drive to the airport.

We checked in and had only sat down near our gate for a few minutes before they announced that our flight to Paris was boarding. I asked Patty, “Are we going to do this or not?” She answered, “We like the town and the apartment. We have someone with experience to do the remodel and manage it. Judy and Harry had done the same and promised to coach us. Everything has lined up. We may never have this opportunity again.”

As we walked to the boarding gate, I called Jean-Christophe and asked him to make an offer on the apartment. When we landed in Paris an hour later, we learned it had been accepted.

Thus began a great adventure for us. What my boss Sheldon told me that spring afternoon more than 30 years before was indeed true: France waited for us. Much happened in the intervening years to put us in the position to buy a small apartment 5,000 miles from home. One thing stands out. Had I not lost the election, we'd have not been in France that January. Patty and I would not have seen the apartment, nor would we have the good friends Harry and Judy have become during the past 10 years. Thanks again, law partner. You beat me fair and square. Doing so changed my life.

RINSE AND REPEAT

Once you've achieved your goal—what's next on your agenda? You've identified one goal. We started slowly. You've put in place the steps necessary to achieve Goal #1. Now you must keep moving. Rinse and repeat, as they say. Knocking off your first goal is your stepping stone to the next accomplishment and then the next. It will work for you if you keep after it.

There's likely more than one step to attain your primary goal. Make each of these steps a stand-alone goal. Eventually, your accomplishments will overlap.

Take, for example, a hard-charging, working 60 hours 5-and-a-half-days a week type practicing lawyer that wants to plan a lifestyle change. Five years from now, our motivated attorney desires to slow down. Putting in 20 hours a week, taking a pottery class, an occasional movie in the afternoon, doing some more board member work, chasing grandkids, and enjoying longer trips make up the initial list of his or her future goals.

Some facets of preparing to pull this off will take longer than others. Each step must take a separate place on the to-do list. The effort it would take to start a pottery class is straightforward, right? Budget the time, declare it a priority, and sign up. A short list of things to do will make up the sub-parts of this goal.

The strategy for reducing the lawyer's commitment to the law firm by two-thirds is more complicated. It won't happen overnight. There will be many items on this goal's list of what needs to be done to make it happen.

These several lists will come together, like the stages you go through to get a deal to closing or to prep for trial. They'll be pursued independently. The pace at which each is accomplished will be different.

Collectively, the components of your plan complement each other.

Where I ended up was not the product of much purposeful planning in my personal life. It was done in earnest for a while, then pushed aside as other life events intervened. Our travel fulfilled dreams but our trips were vacations, not hunts for real estate that would eventually lead to us living part of the year abroad. Some acquaintances we gathered along the way developed into the best of friends. Patty and I asked lots of questions and sought advice resulting in having a stable of trusted advisors and crafts persons who had been vetted by these friends.

As with everything else that ended with us in a good space, it was a confluence of influences that led to that spot in time. Listening to Sheldon's advice, losing the election, and studying French became interrelated. These events stand alone in the scheme of my life but ended up coming together, producing a good result.

FINDING INSPIRATION IN OTHERS

Their goal was 50 by 60: to run a marathon in all 50 states before reaching 60 years of age.

At age 44, Tom Gardner had never run a marathon when his wife Debbie asked if he'd like to give it a try. Debbie had run her first 26-miler in 1989 when she was 30. Tom began training and soon ran his first marathon at Big Sur. During the course of the next six years, they ran seven marathons together.

One day, Tom ran into a friend who was about to run his 50th marathon. They were about the same age. When Tom told his buddy that he wished he had started running when he was younger, the guy said, "I started 10 years ago." Later that day, Tom and Debbie agreed to shoot for running the long-distance race in every state by the time they were 60 years old. They hit their goal at age 57, running 43 marathons in 3 years. When the idea of running a marathon was first brought up, Tom was not a runner, but he told me that "she pulled it out of me, and it was a blast."

Sometime later, Debbie suggested they take a bike ride. Tom's 1983 Centurion was buried in the corner of the garage. He dusted off the old 2-wheeler, pumped up the tires, and off they rode, covering about 30 miles. They found that they enjoyed riding. They took week-long trips, carrying their provisions and gear, and camping along their routes.

When Tom and Debbie were running a marathon in Washington state, they came across a mother and daughter who were biking across the U.S. Debbie and Tom followed the adventures of these two cyclists through their blog. It inspired them to plan their own cross-country cycling trip. In 2018, Debbie and Tom loaded their bikes, camping gear, and provisions on the train and headed to Washington state.

Sixty-seven days and 4,200 biking miles later, they arrived in Bar Harbor, Maine.

One adventure leads to another. While on a ride, they encountered a group of cyclists undertaking the Tour the Divide Challenge, following the Continental Divide from Banff, Alberta, Canada, to Antelope Wells, New Mexico. This inspired them, at 62 years of age, to make the 45-day trip traveling the length of this mountainous path through the United States. The duo recently finished a ride from San Diego, California, to Key West, Florida.

Tom and Debbie have a great partnership when it comes to their adventures as well as in other facets of their lives. Having someone from whom to draw inspiration and to provide a nudge from time to time is a great source of motivation. Look around and see if there is someone you'd enjoy accompanying you as you take on a new experience.

13

Why France, You Ask?

Throughout this book, you've been reading about my goals for retirement from the practice of law—the greatest of which was to land in France for part of each year. I suggested that one of my hobbies was to learn to speak French. I mentioned our many trips to Europe, as well as the purchase of an apartment in the south of France. Well, here's the background for those of you interested in knowing how our personal goals drove the planning and execution of the search for my landing zone.

> "There is never any ending to Paris and the memory of each person who has lived in it differs from that of any other. We always returned to it no matter who we were or how it was changed or with what difficulties, or ease, it could be reached."[1] Paris was always worth it . . .
>
> —*A Moveable Feast,* Ernest Hemingway, American author (1899–1961)

MY VISIT WITH JIM MORRISON

Among many famous artists buried in Paris's famous Père-Lachaise Cemetery is Jim Morrison, one of my favorite rock stars since the 1960s. Morrison keeps eternal company with Edith Piaf, Oscar Wilde, Marcel Proust, and many other celebrities resting in the largest cemetery in the city. His burial was a few days after I joined the army. I visited Jim's grave

[1] Hemingway, Ernest. *A Moveable Feast*. New York: Scribner, 1964.

in the summer of 1972 in a cemetery established by Napoleon Bonaparte. Along with two soldier friends from our base in Bavaria, I took the train to Paris. My pilgrimage to Morrison's grave wasn't the only reason to go to France: while we were in town, we also took in the other sites of the City of Lights.

A cheap hotel on the Boulevard St. Michel provided a base for our expedition. Our days were spent touring while we hit the bars and clubs at night. The budget for my Parisian vacation, meager given what the army was paying at the time, allowed for a diet consisting mostly of beer and hot dogs.

The French served their hot dogs in a baguette. We were impressed. Our meals were provided by sidewalk vendors stationed throughout the city. A baguette was hollowed-out as a part of the chef's production by ramming it a few times on a heated silver post stationed on the vendor's cart. The bun readied, and a skinny, steaming frank was plucked with a pair of tongs from a vat of lukewarm water. It was deftly wriggled into the hole made in the fresh baguette. The vendor passed it over the counter wrapped in a thin white napkin. Such was my first dining experience in France.

I was introduced to the language, France's history, and snippets about the culture of the country while in high school. I had taken three years of French but certainly couldn't speak the language. One of our textbooks, full of dialogue and useful phrases for would-be travelers, was titled "If one day I am in France." At the time, I was parroting phrases from the text in Father Joe Casey's French class; I never thought that I would, one day, try to put its words to work traveling in France. The only people I knew who had been to Europe were my uncles and other men who fought in World War II. No one in our neighborhood had ever vacationed in France.

More interesting to me than math or science were the history courses offered by my high school. My grandfather had served in France during World War I. Dad, my uncles, and my friends' fathers had all been in the military during World War II. I had read much about both wars. By the time I visited Paris, I had already visited many sites in Germany associated with World War II. On that first visit to Paris, I lingered at the memorial plaques honoring resistance fighters who had fallen on that spot during the liberation of Paris in 1944.

The three of us never stopped traipsing about the city. We walked along the Rue de la Ferronnière, where Henri IV met his fate in 1610 and later stood at Napoleon's tomb. We sat at the Medici Fountain in the Jardin du Luxembourg, where Hemingway wrote that he snared pigeons for dinner "in the early days when we were very poor and very happy."[2]

There was a bit of history predating Christopher Columbus's visit to the New World on nearly every block. The feeling of being connected to events of long ago grabbed my attention during my first trip to Paris. It still fascinates me. I was a long way from Durham Drive, where I had lazed away some summer afternoons reading about events that had occurred in Paris, where I now stood.

FIRST IMPRESSIONS

There were other pleasures discovered on my first visit to Paris. There was no such thing as a sidewalk café in 1970s Indianapolis. The clanging of dinnerware on the plates and the clinking of glasses at the outdoor tables was music. I enjoyed the background noise provided by the din of melodic French being chattered at the cafés. Given our soldiers' budgets, we uncharacteristically nursed our beers and lazed occasionally at a café, basking in the experience.

What a totally different world. Growing up, my exposure to dining out was the rare family excursion to the Knights of Columbus Hall (the K of C). The contrast to what I was enjoying as we idled in small cafés doing our best Parisian imitations was stark.

At the K of C, the waitress must have cringed when she saw Mom and Dad leading their brood across the dull tile floor of the dining room. Our routine upon arrival was always the same. We'd barely be seated before my brothers, sisters, and I would ravage the basket of crackers sitting on the table. It would be emptied in seconds. We bigger kids muscled our way to the best crackers, the oblong-shaped packets with sesame seeds or bits of rye baked into the treat—the kind Mom didn't buy. The packages of Ritz and Saltines were scraps left in the basket for our younger and smaller siblings to enjoy. Over Dad's objection, the waitress would replace the original basket that was filled with crumbs and crumpled wrappers with a new and full basket of crackers to squabble over. One could count on at least one glass of water to be spilled on the table during the fray.

Far from Indianapolis in distance and culture, the Parisians with whom I was becoming acquainted, at least through observation, were far more

---

[2] *Id.*

leisurely in their approach to dinner in a restaurant. I had assumed that our occasional chaotic family night out at the K of C was a common experience. Boy was I wrong! In contrast to the K of C dinners, French people sipped their wine and elegantly smoked, cocking their heads at just the proper angle to send the smoke to another table so as not to annoy their companions. There was not a frayed basket of empty cracker wrappers to be seen. Instead, on the tables was a sweating, silver vessel bearing the name of some obscure champagne producer chilling a bottle of wine.

Even the cutlery was put to use differently than at the K of C. I never saw a spoon at work in Paris except for eating ice cream or stirring a cup of coffee. The French went about eating their meals with an upside-down fork in their left hand. The right hand wielded the knife. The blade was used to emphasize a point in the amusing story the holders were telling their dinner companions after carefully cutting a slice of meat. These everyday conventions were managed in a very different fashion. The world at a dinner table in Paris seemed so sophisticated. I decided that I liked this style of dining better than the Friday night battle over crackers at the K of C.

What I really enjoyed about Paris was the hustle, the noise of a big city. There were buses and taxis honking. Motor scooters weaving in and out of traffic. The sidewalks were crowded with people scurrying about. Other than going to Chicago twice and my Washington D.C. trip with the newspaper boys, I had never been anywhere. Our annual one-week family vacations were to visit relatives in Cleveland. The energy of Paris was vibrant and a fresh, new experience. The city left a huge impression on a 19-year-old from Naptown, Indiana. I was already longing to return.

During the three or four days I was in Paris that summer, I was thoroughly taken with things French. I liked the people. At least I thought I did. We didn't really get to know anybody during our brief visit. But they seemed to be living a more charmed life than I believed I would have when I returned to Indiana.

We had a lot of fun on our visit. I had good traveling companions, but traipsing through the galleries of the Louvre or idling at a corner café with two soldiers wasn't what I had in mind for my next trip. I was certain that Patty would love Paris. I hoped that my next visit would be a more romantic adventure— whatever that meant to me at age 19. I was also certain that I had no idea how to finance this future romantic getaway, but I hoped that when I returned, it would be together. After recounting to her the wonders I had discovered during my visit, Patty was easily convinced that a trip to Paris should be in our future. We began sketching out a scheme for our initial *tour de France*.

OUR HALF-BAKED PLAN

I was to be discharged from the army at the end of June 1973. I could stay in Europe with an open plane ticket back to the U.S. courtesy of Uncle Sam. I had been saving half of my paycheck every month, so I had a little money. Patty was going to graduate from high school that May and had also saved some money from babysitting and her part-time job. The timing could not have been better. We decided that when school was over, she would come to Europe, I'd get out of the army, and we'd travel together for the summer. We were excited about our upcoming adventure and mapped out our itinerary through our frequent letters.

The plans for our first visit, though, were snuffed out by a higher authority. It was the early 1970s. I was not quite 20—a high school graduate and soon-to-be veteran with a little bit of money saved. Patty was 18. She worked at a dry cleaner and was soon to be a high school graduate. Our parents, raising Catholic families, weren't too keen on an unmarried, teenage couple traveling together in France or anywhere else on the planet. I can't say that we were shocked when the boom was lowered on our plans.

The *kibosh*, a word Dad loved and used frequently, was put on our upcoming European adventure. In the interest of family harmony and fear of some unknown consequences, we decided the better course was to not defy our parents. Perhaps we caved too easily, but there was no point in rocking the boat. We were determined to find another way to get to France together. Still in Germany, I changed gears and planned to come back to Indiana.

MY AMICABLE SEPARATION FROM THE ARMY

By the spring of 1973, the war in Vietnam was winding down, and the U.S. Army had a glut of soldiers on hand. The government needed to trim back its forces, the fighting forces as well as the nonfighting forces like me. A program was developed offering an early-out for personnel demonstrating a need to return to civilian life before their scheduled Expiration of Term of Service.

I was bored with the military by then. I told the recruiter who called me to his office for the obligatory sales pitch that the army was not my calling. I would not be re-upping for another tour. I was ready to go home. I'd only been in the service for a year and a half, but I was among those provided the opportunity to assist the government in its desire to reduce the military's headcount by leaving before fulfilling my two-year commitment.

A valid reason was required to qualify for this program. Paperwork needed to be submitted. I filled out the necessary form and drafted a letter explaining the reason why I deserved a 90-day drop, the maximum allowed. My plan, I explained, was to start a landscaping business. As I was due to separate from the army on June 30, it would be too late to buy a pickup truck and lawnmower, and develop customers before the mowing season began. It was imperative that I go back to Indiana in the spring and corner my share of the landscaping market before everyone had already contracted with their yard groomer. To deny my request would cause the business I had not yet started to fail, resulting in personal financial hardship. It could also have a negative impact on the Hoosier economy.

My well-polished letter was delivered along with the packet requesting an early out as directed. This was an easy task as it simply required me to leave my desk and carry the material to the office next to mine. The program for our division was administered by a friend working in the office one door down the hall from me.

Not surprisingly, my request was promptly approved. Scooter's Landscape Service was one step closer to reality. On March 9, 1973, the U.S. Army and I separated amicably, and I returned to Indianapolis. Bertermann's Florist, where I had worked during high school delivering flowers, immediately put me back on the payroll. I decided that I never really cared for cutting grass and Scooter's Landscape Service closed before it opened. I doubt the army cared, given that I saved the government three months' salary of one more Army Specialist E-4. The Indiana economy was not negatively affected.

Once back in Indianapolis, Patty and I were together all the time. Much to the disappointment of one of my boyhood friends, we didn't rent an apartment together as we'd planned. I stayed at home saving money as Patty and I prepared to get married. Yes, we would show them that we had a solution to the travel ban: We'd get married. We would no longer require our parents' blessing to travel together.

We've often since joked that we got married the following January so as not to require our parents' blessing to go to Europe. We came a long way from our half-baked plan to backpack around Europe in the summer of 1973 to having a home in France. Our plan germinated for a long time.

14

Waiting It Out to Make It Happen

WHEELS UP, BUT IT TOOK A FEW YEARS

> "Keep away from people who try to belittle your ambitions. Small people always do that, but the really great make you feel that you, too, can become great."[1]
>
> —Mark Twain, American writer (1835–1910)

Our first trip to Europe didn't happen overnight. After our wedding in January of 1974, it took us three years to save enough money for the journey. We scrimped. If we splurged by going out to dinner, we went to a nearby Pizza Hut. Typically, we'd have just enough money to share a pizza and have one beer each. Sometimes, we used a portion of the waitresses' tip to buy a second beer, which we split. We were disciplined and eventually socked enough away to afford a charter flight to Europe.

I had just finished my last college course and was waiting to hear if I had been admitted to law school when we flew to Germany. We visited Frankfurt, Nuremberg, and Ansbach, where I had been stationed. We paid a brief visit to Eastern France and were off to Paris. Patty wrote in her diary that we got on the plane to come home from our two-week vacation with "$9 in cash plus $20 in travelers' checks. If that's not evidence of a good time, I don't know what is."

Many of our early excursions ended with us flying back home flat broke. We'd return on a Sunday evening, and it was back to work on

---

[1] Goodreads. "Mark Twain, Quotes, Quotable Quote." Accessed April 26, 2023. https://www.goodreads.com/quotes/2528-keep-away-from-people-who-try-to-belittle-your-ambitions.

Monday morning. We would not be flush again until payday at the end of the week, so visits to the grocery store had to wait. Our remedy was to invite ourselves to Patty's parents' house or pop by Mom and Dad's around 6:00 p.m. during that first week back in the United States.

ANNUAL VISITS

Our first trip to Europe inspired us to plan our next visit. Our interest in returning to Europe never waned. We would save throughout the year to have enough money for a summer trip to Europe. Mostly we traveled to France. In the early days, we stayed in cheap hotels. The buildings were well-worn and the owners friendly. If the lumpy beds weren't enough to disrupt a good night's sleep, the traffic noise outside the thin windows did the trick. On the first four or five excursions, you'd have found us in Paris, dining at an inexpensive Chinese restaurant, maybe with a beer in hand. Meals at a classy French bistro and a bottle of wine would come later.

The more we visited France, the more we enjoyed being there. Though we traveled to other countries, Patty and I both loved our time in the land of the Gauls. Much like my first visit with army buddies, we found the people to be friendly and the relaxed lifestyle appealing. At home, we were both burning the candle at both ends, which caused us to take notice that the French worked to live. Unlike Americans, the French, we learned, did not live to work. We fell into that mode during our short annual stays. Then, Patty and I would return to our exhausting schedules for most of the next 50 weeks of the year.

Even in later years, when we were able to return to the United States not completely broke, we were frugal. We sought out inexpensive and thus uncomfortable charter flights. We rented the puniest and least expensive vehicles, which left us feeling as if we were standing still when Porsches and Mercedes whizzed by on the speed-limitless Autobahn.

The hotels became less worn as a good night's sleep became more important. We graduated from Chinese food, finding seats in French bistros and nicer restaurants. We had been 24 and 22 years old when we took our first trip: as we got older, our tastes matured along with our budget.

We traveled to France more often after we purchased our first French apartment in 2012. For the first 35 years, our trips were rarely longer than two weeks. As I reduced my commitment to the law firm, we increased the length of our stays in France. Eventually, we sold our small apartment and got out of the rental business. We purchased a bigger apartment that was more comfortable during longer stays. Two weeks grew to three and three to four. In 2017, we were in France for 12 weeks during two visits. We spent nine months in Provence during the pandemic.

WHAT ABOUT THE KIDS?

Our view was—and continues to be—that parents and kids should enjoy a vacation *from* each other from time to time. It's good for everyone to have a break from the household rules every so often. We were married for 10 years before our first child's birth. After we were married and before Sean was born, I went to college and law school. I had practiced law for nearly four years. Patty had been to beauty school, built up her business, and had owned her salon for six years. By 1984, when Sean joined the family, we were traveling better than in our early trips. The lumpy beds and Chinese restaurants were mostly behind us. We were determined not to stop seeing the world for the sole reason that we now had a child.

After our first trip in 1977, and up until 2012, we visited France probably 35 times. I know that this is an accurate count as Patty kept a diary of each excursion. She kept track of every expense, the names of our hotels and restaurants, and the cost of every purchase. Normally we were gone between 10 days and 2 weeks. When our kids were in high school, we managed several three-week trips on which they came along. Over the years, we've explored almost every province and corner of the country. I've lost track of how many times we've been to Paris.

Going to new places was important to us and having children didn't need to stop us. When Sean was a month old, he accompanied us on a ski trip to Colorado. He stayed with our neighbors for a week when he was five months old after we found a good deal and made an impromptu trip to Italy. That raised a few eyebrows.

After daughters Maureen and Colleen joined the household, we kept our practice of getting away together once a year when we were financially able and our schedules permitted. It's good for children to enjoy the freedom provided by a lenient babysitter. And some of ours were lenient. We were periodically quizzed by well-intentioned good friends who wondered about leaving three children behind while we went off on vacation. Parents, at least we at the time, need a respite from the day-to-day program. Early on, we'd justify our annual sojourn by telling them our relationship was important, too; the kids would leave us one day and it will be just us. I'm not sure this rationalization was always accepted by some friends who questioned what they may have perceived to be our lack of commitment as parents. After all, weren't we annually abandoning our three kids for a week or two?

In the end, the children left us behind as predicted. Sean, Maureen, and Colleen all turned 18 and went away to college. Except for a brief stint by Sean, they never came back to live at home. We've discerned no scars or inadequacies caused by having babysitters during our travels, not even after a week at the neighbors' when Sean was five months old.

For years, we debated as to when our kids would be old enough to join us in France. My observation of taking trips with young children is that it is a trip. It is not a vacation. Why pay to transport our daily lives to a different location? Diapers still needed to be changed, bedtimes had to be observed, and meals put on the table at regularly set intervals. Not that we didn't have fun family trips, but a five-year-old couldn't care less about the Louvre. There were plenty of beaches in the United States to enjoy without involving a transatlantic flight as means of travel. We postponed exposing our children to Europe until they were teenagers.

Part of our parenting philosophy was that it was essential to maintain our relationship separate from that of the kids. When our children were young, we had a babysitter scheduled almost every week. One of the four neighbor girls was set to come to our house every Saturday evening. If we chose not to go out to dinner, we'd pay them anyway. As an older sitter developed a social life or found a boyfriend and began to refuse our babysitting requests, we'd move down the line, and her younger sister would take the job. This worked until the youngest girl was a year older than Sean. The kids said it seemed a bit "weird" to have her babysit a near-peer in age. They were right. We began to allow the kids to carry on without a sitter on Saturday nights when we went out.

There was only one instance where a sitter left us hanging during a trip. Patty went with me to San Francisco, where I had a conference. Sean was off to college and the girls were in high school. We were comfortable that they could care for themselves and get to school, but we wanted someone in the house with them at night. As we settled into our hotel on the West Coast, I called to check in and let them know we had made it safely. It was late in Indianapolis, and our daughters were watching TV. I asked to talk to the sitter. Maureen responded that: "Grandma went home. She said we'd be just fine." Without telling us, my mom elected to babysit long distance from my parents' condo a few miles away. Mom was right: the girls got along just fine.

MAKING FRIENDS

Even during our early European adventures, although our language skills were elementary, we managed to strike up friendships with some of the locals. Several times we were exchanging pleasantries in a restaurant where the tables were arranged close together, resulting in an invitation to our new acquaintances' home for an after-dinner coffee. We were asked to several parties and invited to hang out with other travelers we met in hotel lobbies. Patty and I also developed some lasting friendships with couples we've met in our travels.

During one of our early trips, we spent a week at a small hotel on a Mediterranean beach near Sanary-sur-Mer. Michel and Genevieve were a couple our ages running the Hotel Solviou. They treated us like family, insisting we eat dinner with them after the other guests were fed and sent on their way. Over the course of our several visits to the Solviou, they introduced us to mussels and oysters, *pastis* and rosé, and to the music of Michel Sardou and France Gall. Michel taught us how to play *boules (petanque)* in the Solviou's dusty courtyard after a day at the beach. We learned words our French teachers had neglected to share with us.

We've kept in touch with Genevieve and Michel since 1979, corresponding via postcards and letters. Sadly, Michel passed away before he could retire and enjoy the life for which he had been preparing.

Now we email or drop notes to Genevieve and her brothers on Facebook. We have lunch with Genevieve, her children, grandchildren, brothers, and other family members at her home at least once a year. After our meal, we play *boules* while Genevieve and her brother Philippe teach us more words that our French teachers have failed to incorporate into our vocabulary.

More recently, a friend introduced me to a bicycling club in our town. I signed on and now cycle two or three days a week through the Vaucluse countryside with riders about my age. I've been accepted and am referred to as "our American" in the group's Facebook posts. Those friendships have evolved and Patty and I now have dinner at the homes of new French friends.

CHANCE ENCOUNTER AND A LASTING FRIENDSHIP

Our trips have been enriched by the people who came into our lives along the road. We have, often through happenstance, met people who often re-entered our lives beyond our initial encounters.

For example, I was struggling to secure our rented boat in a canal lock during our first such trip in 1995. We were celebrating Patty's birthday by piloting a small boat along the Canal de Bourgogne. An Austrian couple on their boat was in the lock with us. They coached us through our first experience with ropes, knots, and our boat rocking as the lock furiously emptied. During the next four days, we cruised at the same pace as Hanna and Robert. We had lunches together and rode our bikes to visit sites along our route.

Since that first encounter, we've traveled canals and rivers with Hanna and Robert on several boat trips.

Every few years, we met for long weekends somewhere in Europe. We've twice been their guests in Vienna, and Hanna has come to our homes in Indianapolis and in Provence for visits. I had a personal guide in Robert when he escorted me through the *Heeresgeschichtliches Museum* (Military History Institute) in Vienna. Robert and I have had many interesting conversations about our lives as well as about the Romans, World War II, and our fathers' participation on opposite sides of the conflict.

On Saturday mornings in L'Isle sur la Sorgue, several of us regularly meet up with a French friend and his dog at 8:20. Our walks take us along the River Sorgue. Ollie roams off-leash while Serge, his owner, puffs on his cigarette. This is no power walk. It is a leisurely stroll in the country. We chat about world politics and music. Along the course, we are schooled on what the French celebrities living in the area have done to annoy or ingratiate themselves with the locals. Sometimes we end up back at Serge's home for a cup of tea and a croissant. When not in France, these are some of the moments I miss most.

FROM TOURISTS TO COMMUNITY MEMBERS

Developing a social life became one of the drivers for eventually settling in one place in France. This was not an easy decision. We enjoyed traveling throughout the country. The different regions of France have their own distinct cultures. There was always something new to see as we covered the different corners of the country. Some of our French friends teasingly tell us that we've seen more of their country than they have. Ultimately, we decided that it was important to have a steady group of friends if we were going to expand our stays in Europe beyond our three- or four-week trips. Otherwise, we would always be tourists, never having the experience of really living in France.

The friends we spend time with while in Provence come from all over the world. There are a few other Americans sprinkled among the Moroccan, Irish, Scots, Brits, Australians, and French people that we now run around with. Local shopkeepers, friends of friends, and sometimes tourists we meet at the market have become a part of our social life in small-town France. The decision to plant roots has been a good one, but it hasn't prevented us from packing a bag, walking to the train station, and jumping off on a journey to another part of France or Europe we wish to visit or revisit.

We've established residency in France, as well. By virtue of my Irish grandparents, I have dual nationalities: American and Irish. I have European Union and American passports. Patty, as the spouse of an EU citizen, has a *titre de sejour*, her French residency card. This status permits us to stay in Europe beyond the 90 out of 180 days Americans may visit without a visa. It has also eased our border crossings a few times.[2]

LEARNING FRENCH

Early on we realized that learning to speak the language would enrich our travels. We could order a meal and a hotel room, and we could exchange pleasantries using what French we'd each picked up in our high school and college courses. But memorizing dialogue to repeat in class to Father Joe and making our way in conversation at a party in Paris were two different things.

As a young woman, Germaine Phillips married an American soldier at the end of World War II. She moved to Indianapolis with Walter and taught French from her home. Once a week, beginning in the late 1970s, Patty and

---

[2] If you are interested in more information about becoming an Irish citizen by descent, visit Ireland's Department of Foreign Affairs: https://www.dfa.ie/citizenship/born-abroad/registering-a-foreign-birth/.

I drove 45 minutes to the other side of town for our classes with Germaine. I frequently drove directly from my office and met Patty at Germaine's. We slowly began to really learn the language.

Showing up without having done my homework became a running joke. French class was important to me and was set in stone on my calendar. Writing out the conjugations of verbs and filing out the worksheets Germaine expected of us became increasingly more difficult for me to accomplish. Patty was far better at the homework than I was. I was busy at work and did not take the time for *les devoirs*—my homework.

These classes went on for a number of years. After Sean was born, he would sometimes accompany us. Husband Walter enjoyed having a little companion and would play with Sean while we worked on our language skills with Germaine. As it became more difficult to juggle work, family, and nearly an hour's drive to her home, we eventually gave up our first formal French lessons.

When my plan for leaving the full-time practice of law came online, we began to spend more time in France. While at home, with some of my day freed up from the firm, we began studying with another French woman in Indianapolis. Patty and I signed on and began meeting with Cécile Carre for weekly classes. This, coupled with our more frequent and extended visits to the country, boosted our proficiency significantly. I worked with Cécile for three or four years. When in Indianapolis, I still visit with her if she has an opening in her schedule so that I have someone to chat with and correct my pronunciation and choice of verb tenses. I still don't do my homework. I'll never be a native speaker, but I get along well.

Patty now enjoys three classes per week. She has instructors in France and still takes her weekly class with Cécile in Indianapolis. Zoom is a wonderful tool for matters beyond office team meetings. Patty has her weekly French classes, no matter where we may be.

Periodically, I threaten to take up another weekly French language session. I have complained to French friends about my desire to improve, to have a better accent, and to not sometimes confuse verb tenses.

Our friend Franck tells me not to worry about it, "We understand you, Kevin."

Our annual two-week visits weren't enough to pick up the language, and it was years before we were able to stretch our two-week trips to longer periods. Over the years, we've worked with these various other tutors and have been part of several group lessons. I also took a class through an adult education program. I try to read something in French every week. The cassette tapes I listened to in my car driving to the office in Greenfield have been replaced by a French podcast through my earbuds as I take my morning walks.

Over 40-some years, we have become proficient. Patty and I visit with friends who speak no English. We've navigated issues at the bank, purchased real estate, and dealt with contractors and repairmen working on our apartment. Most enjoyably, we now have the skills to spend time with friends who do not speak English. We can chat with the vendors at Provence's open-air markets. We continue to make new friends. Now that we can communicate, we are able to say that we legitimately like France, in part, because of the people. We get along well *en français*.

LANDING WITH OUR FEET IN TWO PONDS

As I was humming along, focusing on my career, other interests were quietly being nurtured. The pace of development, as well as learning about and experiencing France, was much different than my work life. It was leisurely relative to the more hard-driven interest—and need—in developing in my profession. On the France front, there was no goal in mind, unlike my quest to be a good attorney. It was just something Patty and I both enjoyed.

I agree with Hemingway: traveling to and in France is always worth it. We always return no matter how easy or difficult it may have been at a particular time of life. Our relationship with France has changed, as have we. It became more than an annual vacation trip: it developed into a passion. The on-and-off French classes we took, our two-week-a-year visits, meeting Europeans, and staying in contact with them until our next visit morphed into an appreciation for the lifestyle and culture.

We would finish one excursion and begin planning the next. It was comforting to have the next visit on the calendar, even if it was 11 months out. As so much time and effort were invested in my desire to be a good lawyer, developing other skills and interests were secondary. For most of our lives, the idea that we could or would live in Europe was a pipe dream—something other people do. Not that it wasn't discussed, particularly when sitting in a sidewalk café, sipping a glass of wine as the world in France went by.

The route to having a life in another country ran parallel to my professional life. This desire was under the surface, running in the background. There were certain periods when my professional life was all-consuming. Everything else was tuned out when preparing for and then engaging in a lengthy trial, writing and re-writing briefs, or developing a legal ethics program. But when not immersed in time-consuming projects, thoughts about France or being proficient in the French language were percolating.

The confluence of changing my role at the law firm and having the opportunity to spend more time in France snuck up on us. It was another of the wonderful unintended consequences of giving up my partnership in the firm and consciously reducing my commitment to work as a lawyer.

Forty years of professional life eventually merged with our personal interests. I worked less and traveled more. Patty and I did so intending to be more than tourists. Now, the acquired knowledge of the country and the language we'd picked up in bits and pieces over 45-plus years is being put to good use.

Searching for a better way to express the fact that "If I can do it, you can do it" became frustrating for me. The concept is simple and straightforward. I don't believe the phrase is overused. I'm content to go with it like so many others before me. I do want to be clear that I state this as a fact. You can do it. I'm your Exhibit A. Of course, you will need to define your own "it." Then you'll need to get to work.

STEVE STRAWBRIDGE: LAWYER TURNED PAINTER

It's never too late to return to a past passion given up earlier in life for the pragmatic pursuit of a career. Steve Strawbridge was an accomplished lawyer with a long and distinguished career. After he hung up his suit and tie for the last time, he took up painting portraits of his grandchildren as a hobby. He soon graduated to offering to paint portraits of his friends' children and grandchildren using photographs as his models. Steve refused offers of payment, asking that recipients of his work make a donation to the Little Sisters of the Poor whose mission is to offer a home to the neediest elderly. Steve and his spouse Jan added a studio in a spare room where he paints every day. Now, a few years into his retirement as a lawyer, Steve is selling some of his artwork. He's taking art classes to hone his talent and learn new techniques. His work has been admitted in juried exhibitions.

I was still spending most of my time lawyering when Steve had left work. Patty and I asked how he was enjoying his retirement. I was in the midst of my search for what's next and interested in his take on life without partner meetings and accounting for his time in six-minute increments.

Steve told us he was keeping busy, in part, by painting. I told him I thought that he was too old for ladders and asked what he would do when he finished painting the house?

Steve then pulled out from under the table some of the portraits he had brought to show us. I was amazed at the quality of his work. I have known Steve since we were in high school and didn't know he had this talent. I knew the hours he previously had devoted to his work, family, the weekly poker night at the country club, and his golf game. I asked how he became an artist so quickly.

Well, it turns out that at about age 13, Steve was awarded a scholarship to John Heron Art School in Indianapolis. He clearly had innate artistic talent that began to develop in Saturday morning classes when he was a boy. But once high school came along, Steve's art classes were over. He set aside his paints and canvases while he earned his high school diploma and college degrees, and then pursued his legal career.

More than 40 years later, Steve revisited the artistic interest that he'd set aside when he started high school. He now has the time to exercise his talent and is doing something fulfilling.[3]

Maybe there are interests you abandoned in favor of making a living and raising a family that you wish to take up again. Take a moment to consider what you need to do to awaken a dormant talent and engage in something you enjoyed before the demands of life interfered.

---

3 Strawbridge Studio. "About Steven J. Strawbridge, Esq." Accessed April 26, 2023. https://www.strawbridgestudio.com/about.

SUMMARY

> **"You have as many lives as you have possibilities. There are lives where you make different choices. And those choices lead to different outcomes. If you had done just one thing differently, you would have a different life story."[1]**
>
> —*Matt Haig,* The Midnight Library

It was just luck that Jim had my résumé that led to my first job. It was happenstance that the Indiana Legislature passed a statute that changed my course with the law firm. I still don't know with certainty why my orders were changed from Vietnam to Germany. Had our long-time host's mother-in-law picked a different date for her visit, we may not have reacquainted ourselves with Provence. Turn around the management committee election, and we'd never have been in France and discovered the apartment we purchased.

An important factor contributing to finding myself at this place in life is that I asked for help. Dad helped me collect newspaper money from Mr. Creek. The career advice Sheldon Breskow dished out turned out to be spot on. Most people, attorneys, in particular, will be glad to share their advice with you. You only have to ask. Asking Monica Foster to introduce me to Dick Kiefer was simple enough. It totally changed the trajectory of my career.

I had the good fortune to practice in government, in a small firm, and as a sole practitioner. I helped develop a law firm, worked in a large firm, and picked up law firm management experience along the way. My

---

[1] Haig, Matt. *The Midnight Library*. New York: Viking Press, 2020.

involvement in each of these operations provided experience and bits of knowledge on which to build. They made me better at the next stage.

Similarly, in my life outside of the office, things that interested me had to wait. Avocations were put on hold. I left them to percolate under the surface of my day-to-day life, forced to wait for their moment.

Thirty-one years after picking Greenfield over Paris, we purchased an apartment in Provence. As I ratcheted down my hours and working remotely became more common at the law firm, we increased our time in L'Isle-sur-la-Sourge, a small town in the Vaucluse. Our two-week vacations grew into one-month stays. I served my last client from France during the course of a 10-week stay. As I write, we've been at our apartment in Provence for five months. We have no return ticket.

It doesn't matter how well you have planned—or not planned—your career up to this moment. As J.M. Barrie suggested, things happen to us without our noticing that they ever happened. You've arrived at this point. You are here. You need to start your next chapter from today. Be strategic. Get to where you wish to be in a more efficient way than I was able to do.

It is easy to stagnate. Complacency requires little energy. You can operate in your comfort zone, turn out good work, and make a decent living. Your skill level will rise, but it may be difficult to keep doing the same thing forever. The world will change around you and your interests will change. Outside the office, what thrilled you at age 30 may not be fulfilling when you're 50. You need to keep looking ahead and do some planning. If not, you could be left behind.

In the course of our lives, there are times when opportunity has come knocking. Often, we're so caught up in the day-to-day management of our business or life that we let it pass us by. The "I'm busy" mantra interferes with setting aside a moment to evaluate a situation that may present an opportunity for us. Remember, being busy is a choice.

Lawyers possess different talents. Our abilities at attracting and retaining clients vary. Fields of practice can be very different. These and other influences impact a lawyer's bargaining power with the firm.

In almost any size operation, it is sometimes difficult to construct a scheme for a partner to move on. It's a challenge to find a plan readily agreed upon as being fair to the law firm, the heading-to-retirement senior partner, as well as the younger partners.

There will be obstacles along your journey. Distractions will postpone some of your steps. At times you will think progress is too slow. The hill is too steep. Perhaps without being conscious of it, you are methodically adding to your base of knowledge, which will be critical to success. Accomplishments, minor and extraordinary, are being added to your experience. It's just not always obvious until one day, you put it all together.

In driver's education, we were told to stop, look, and listen as we approached a railroad crossing. This is also great career advice. The cues that periodically cross our desks require a moment's pause. Sure, you are going to miss some of these cues and misinterpret others., but if you stop for a moment in a busy day, you will catch yourself thinking, "I need to pursue that a little further."

Thank the people that looked out for you. They will be flattered that you remembered their contributions to your success. Lots of people looked out for me on the path. A few passed on before I realized the value of the help they had given me. I'm sorry I wasn't as observant at age 21 to see that by not promoting me, George was helping me avoid diverting from my plan. I'm grateful that I had time with Sheldon and Jim before they died to let them know that I was appreciative of the opportunity and guidance each of them gave to me. You will not regret making a call on someone who helped get you where you are today.

Keep in mind that you have only yourself to please when it comes to making a decision about a major change in your lifestyle. That's not to say you don't confide in those you love. For many, a change in careers, cutting back your hours, or retiring is a joint decision. If you are happy and leading a fruitful life, those you are closest to will be equally satisfied. Tune out the naysayers. You've got this.

Risks are required. There are no exceptions. Camping in your comfort zone with your head down is easy. Unlike Lindbergh, you're not crossing the Atlantic Ocean using stars and a compass to get you to the other side. A foray here or there that doesn't work out only adds to your bank of experience. You won't have to ditch into the sea.

Don't sell yourself short. If you are in a firm, be honest and bold—but not crazy—when you tell your partners that you want a personalized exit program. You will not be offered more pay for less work. Propose a deal the firm can't refuse. Scale back your financial expectations to meet your new commitment to yourself, which means less time in the office.

If you are a sole practitioner, you have a valuable asset—the firm you built. Your mentorship and fair treatment of those lawyers you brought aboard will be rewarded when you devise your exit strategy. Your goodwill won't be forgotten when the time comes to fund your reduced time at the firm or full retirement. Don't discount the value of the hard work you put in to create and grow your law firm.

Get your money act together. With professional help, you will discover that your dream of slowing down, changing careers, or hanging it up is within reach. Do not be discouraged by cookie-cutter financial plans. Construct your own financial vision with someone who knows what they are doing—and with whom you enjoy working. Start forming your personal financial program now. Revisit it at appropriate intervals and prepare for your next phase. It will be here before you know it.

I've shared with you much about my formative years; dreams dashed, detours taken, and now where Patty and I have landed. Telling you about our lives is the tool I chose. There are other methods to convey this message. For me, this was the best way I know to share my ideas to get you started.

The paths to this point in time we've taken are different. You surely didn't grow up on Durham Drive. Likely you were not a former candy man who scored a D in contracts. My collection of rejection letters from law firms stacks higher than yours.

Our experiences were not the same. You never hid in a forsythia bush waiting to surprise Mr. Creek with "collect for *The Times*" before dawn. Your parents and my parents had different styles for bringing us along. The teachers and bosses you have encountered were not the same ones that helped shape my life.

The things that interest each of us may be worlds apart. Not everyone cares to speak a second language or live in a foreign land. There are lots of things to do other than write, sit on the beach, or play tour guide.

From time to time I hear, "I want to be you when I grow up." It's mostly in my conversations with friends and younger acquaintances. Most of them are in the throes of raising young children, financing college educations, and working their way up the ladder. "Well, I wanted to be me when I was your age, and that was not all that long ago," is my reply.

I've tried my last case and am quite happy to say so. As I said at the beginning of this book, I have no interest in retiring. I've much more to accomplish.

Improve the odds of being the most satisfied *you*. This book is about the possible. Don't wait around as I did. Start chasing your dream today by committing the time to plot your course. Take some time to plan to do what you most enjoy now. Do it with someone. Time is not an abundant commodity. You will never regret your efforts.

Over these pages, I hope that you have found something that moves you down the road. Perhaps something you've heard before but shrugged off. "Come, my friends. 'Tis not too late to seek a newer world. Push off . . ."[2] Now is the time to give it a go.

You don't want to be me, do what I do, or live like I live. I put these stories together, hoping that you will be inspired, get you thinking, and kick-start you to envision an enjoyable future on whatever path you choose. I can't live your best life. You can't have mine. It's up to you to paint your own picture of what your life will be like after the bar. It won't look like what's on my canvas. I hope what you draw for yourself is thoroughly satisfying to you.

[2] Tennyson, Lord Alfred. "Ulysses." In *Poems*. London: Moxon, 1842.

A

Appendix: List of Things I Want to Do

June 2007

- Freedom to travel to Colorado and Mississippi total of two to four times per year
- Freedom to travel to Europe spring and fall for three to four weeks
- Enjoy home and Indy by free weekends and evenings—enhanced by some four-day weeks
- Visit Romania
- Work on research for family tree—perhaps trip back to Salt Lake City—Mormon resources
- Visit Ireland
- See Mary in Canada—trip to Midland, Ontario
- Visit Jim and Sandy in Arizona
- Ski one to two times per year
- Weekend or several-day retreat at Milford or St. Meinrad
- Improve French language capability
- Learn Spanish
- Maybe learn German
- Learn guitar
- Write practical ethics text for practicing Indiana lawyer
- Publish more articles on legal topics—maybe have a column
- Find outlet for other writing projects
- Ditch practice of criminal law except to mentor and advise
- Develop business consulting practice for lawyers
- Be more versed in field of ethics by study/reading
- Find future role in Indiana State Bar Association
- Find role in Indianapolis Bar Association
- Exercise—cardio three to four times per week; lift two to three times per week; bike in to work one to three times per week
- Hone practice to legal ethics, defending lawyers and some family law

- Consider pitching the mentoring role to Bingham
- Establish consistent plan to meet/know more lawyers and staff at Bingham
- See more Indy sites
- Ride bike more
- Get new bike
- Work on John's campaign for Congress
- Putter in yard
- See more movies
- Take a sabbatical
- Take classes at a university—French history
- Photography class
- Plant garden
- Sailboat trip in the Caribbean
- More flexibility—i.e., more free time than work time in a week/month/year

B

Appendix: Cost of Living Worksheet[1]

	Year 1	Year 2 Est.	Difference
INCOME			
Salaries, Wages & Tips			
Interest Income			
Dividends			
Refunds/Reimbursements			
Transfer from Savings			
Social Security			
Other (e.g., from rental properties)			
Total INCOME			
HOME EXPENSES			
HELOC			
Electricity			
Utilities: Gas/Water/Sewer/Trash			

[1] There are many on-line resources providing Budget Worksheets. I started with a template called Vertex42 and tailored it to our needs. See the Household Budget Worksheet for Excel at https://www.vertex42.com/ExcelTemplates/monthly-household-budget.html.

Recycling fees			
Cell Phones			
Cable TV/Internet/Home Phone			
Alarm Service			
Furnishings/Appliances (new)			
Lawn Care			
Household			
Maintenance			
Hardware			
Pest Control			
Pool Service & Repairs			
Other			
Total HOME EXPENSES			
DAILY LIVING			
Groceries			
Personal Supplies			
Clothing (new)			
Home Cleaning Services			
Dining/Eating Out			
Dry Cleaning			
Beauty Products			

Trainer/Massages			
Cash/Misc. Spending			
Other			
Total DAILY LIVING			
TRANSPORTATION			
Vehicle Payments			
Fuel			
Bus/Taxi/Train Fare			
Repairs			
Registration/License			
Other			
Total TRANSPORTATION			
HEALTH			
Doctor			
Medicine/Drugs			
Optical			
Labs			
Dentists			
Total HEALTH			

INSURANCE			
Auto			
Health			
Home Owners			
Life			
Disability			
Total INSURANCE			
CHARITY/GIFTS			
Gifts Given			
Charitable Donations			
Religious Donations			
Kids			
Total CHARITY/GIFTS			
EDUCATION			
Tuition			
Other			
Total EDUCATION			
BUDGET SUMMARY			
Total Income			
Total Expenses			
Net			

SAVINGS			
Emergency Fund			
Transfer to Savings			
Retirement (401k, IRA)			
Investments			
College			
Other			
Total SAVINGS			
OBLIGATIONS			
Property Tax			
Federal Taxes			
State/Local Taxes			
Accounting/Personal Financial Planner Fees			
Other			
Total OBLIGATIONS			
BUSINESS EXPENSES			
Total BUSINESS EXPENSES			

ENTERTAINMENT			
Videos/DVDs			
Sirius			
Wine			
French Class			
Movies/Theater			
Concerts			
Books			
Writing			
Film/Photos			
Sports			
Outdoor Recreation			
Toys/Gadgets			
Computers			
Total ENTERTAINMENT			
SUBSCRIPTIONS			
Newspaper			
Magazines			
Club Membership			
Gym Membership			
Other			
Total SUBSCRIPTIONS			

VACATION			
Transportation (air, train, etc.) & travel			
Lodging			
Food			
Rental Car			
Entertainment			
Other			
Total VACATION			
MISCELLANEOUS			
Bank Fees			
Postage			
Dues			
Other			
Other			
Other			
Total MISCELLANEOUS			

ABOUT THE AUTHOR

Kevin McGoff is an author, travel writer, speaker, and lawyer. During his career Kevin worked for a state agency, ran a solo practice, and started a law firm. Later he served as General Counsel to a large mid-west firm. As he looked to other horizons Kevin crafted a plan with his law firm's management allowing him to wind down his career while developing new skills. He retired from the practice of law in 2021.

Kevin is an award winning travel writer, avid cyclist, and inveterate traveler. He developed a successful program to complement *Find Your Landing Zone: Life Beyond The Bar* designed to motivate lawyers and other professionals to progress from thinking about what's next in life to creating a personal plan to make it happen.

Married to his wife Patty for 49 years, they have three children, five grandchildren, and no pets. Patty and Kevin live in the South of France and Indiana.

Visit Kevin online at https://surlaroutekm.com/about/ or drop him a note at kevin.mcgoff1@gmail.com.

BIBLIOGRAPHY

There were many books and articles that passed through my fingers as I set out to figure out where I wanted to land. The following are some of the resources I found helpful, inspirational, or contain snippets of information I liked.

Bauer, Gary P. *Hire and Retire: A Plan for a Continuing Income Stream in Retirement from Any Practice*. Chicago: ABA Book Publishing, 2019.

Berson, Susan. *The Lawyer's Retirement Planning Guide, Second Edition*. Chicago: ABA Book Publishing, 2014.

Brooks, Albert C. *From Strength to Strength: Finding Success, Happiness, and Deep Purpose in the Second Half of Life*. New York: Portfolio, 2022.

Frankl, Viktor E. *Man's Search for Meaning*. Boston: Beacon Press, 1959.

Soled, Jay A. *A Lawyer's Guide to Retirement and Lifetime Planning: Estate Planning Strategies*. Chicago: ABA Book Publishing, 2002.

Sharp, Cynthia. *The Lawyer's Guide to Financial Planning*. Chicago: ABA Book Publishing, 2015.

Zelinski, Ernie J. *How to Retire Happy, Wild, and Free: Retirement Wisdom That You Won't Get from Your Financial Advisor*. Edmonton: Visions Inspirational Publishing, 2021.